DREAMS

**Tonight's Answers
for Tomorrow's Questions**

EDGAR CAYCE'S WISDOM FOR THE NEW AGE

General Editor: Charles Thomas Cayce
Project Editor: A. Robert Smith

Dreams: Tonight's Answers for Tomorrow's Questions,
   Mark Thurston

Awakening Your Psychic Powers, Henry Reed

Reincarnation: Claiming Your Past, Creating Your Future,
   Lynn Elwell Sparrow

DREAMS

Tonight's Answers
for Tomorrow's Questions

MARK THURSTON

With a Foreword by Charles Thomas Cayce

1817

Harper & Row, Publishers, San Francisco

Cambridge, Hagerstown, New York, Philadelphia, Washington
London, Mexico City, São Paulo, Singapore, Sydney

To Morton Blumenthal, who sixty years ago had the wisdom more often than anyone else to ask for dream interpretation readings from Edgar Cayce; and to Harmon Bro, whose research, scholarship, and writing about the Cayce dream readings has inspired me and thousands of others.

DREAMS: *Tonight's Answers for Tomorrow's Questions.* Copyright © 1988 by Mark Thurston. All rights reserved. Printed in the United States of America. No part of this book may be used or reproduced in any manner whatsoever without written permission except in the case of brief quotations embodied in critical articles and reviews. For information address Harper & Row, Publishers, Inc., 10 East 53rd Street, New York, NY 10022. Published simultaneously in Canada by Fitzhenry & Whiteside, Limited, Toronto.

FIRST EDITION

Library of Congress Cataloging-in-Publication Data
Thurston, Mark A.
    Dreams: tonight's answers for tomorrow's questions.

    (Edgar Cayce's wisdom for the new age)
    Bibliography: p.
    Includes index.
    1. Dreams. 2. Cayce, Edgar, 1877–1945. 3. Dreams—
Dictionaries. I. Title. II. Series.
BF1091.T46 1988   135'.3   87-46230
ISBN: 0-06-250864-4 (pbk.)

88 89 90 91 92   FG   10 9 8 7 6 5 4 3 2 1

CONTENTS

Foreword by Charles Thomas Cayce vii
Introduction: Awakening to Your Dreams xi

PART I: WHAT IS A DREAM?   1

1   The Mysterious Wisdom of Your Dreams   3
2   The Anatomy of a Dream   15
3   Remembering Your Dreams   23

PART II: INTERPRETING YOUR DREAMS   35

4   Getting Started on Dream Interpretation   37
5   Finding the Simple Story Line   47
6   How the Dream Fits Your Life   62
7   The Meaning of Dream Symbols   78

**PART III: PSYCHIC AND
SPIRITUAL DREAMS   91**

8   The Reality of Your Dream Experiences   93

9   Dreams of Power: Lucidity, Astral Travel, and Out-of-Body   103

10   ESP and Dream Guidance   118

PART IV: THE EDGAR CAYCE DREAM SYMBOL DICTIONARY   139

Selected Bibliography   218
Index   219

FOREWORD

IT IS A TIME in the earth when people everywhere seek to know more of the mysteries of the mind, the soul," said my grandfather, Edgar Cayce, from an unconscious trance from which he demonstrated a remarkable gift for clairvoyance.

His words are prophetic even today, as more and more Americans in these unsettled times are turning to psychic explanations for daily events. For example, according to a national survey by the National Opinion Research Council nearly half of American adults today believe they have been in contact with someone who has died, a figure twice that of ten years ago. Two-thirds of all adults say they have had an ESP experience; ten years ago that figure was only one-half.

Every culture throughout history has made note of its own members' gifted powers beyond the five senses. These rare individuals held special interest because they seemed able to provide solutions to life's pressing problems. And America in the twentieth century is no exception.

Edgar Cayce was perhaps the most famous and most carefully documented psychic of our time. He began to use his unusual abilities when he was a young man, and from then on for over 40 years he would, usually twice a day, lie on a couch, go into a sleeplike state, and respond to questions. Over 14,000 of these discourses, called readings, were carefully transcribed by his secretary and preserved by the Edgar Cayce Foundation in Virginia Beach, Virginia. These psychic readings continue to provide inspiration, insight, and help with healing to tens of thousands of people.

Having only an eighth-grade education, Edgar Cayce lived a plain and simple life by the world's standards. As early as his childhood in Hopkinsville, Kentucky, however, he sensed that he had psychic ability. While alone one day he had a vision of a woman who told him he would have unusual power to help people. He also related experiences of "seeing" dead relatives. Once, while struggling with school lessons, he slept on his spelling book and awakened knowing the entire contents of the book.

As a young man he experimented with hypnosis to treat a recurring throat problem that caused him to lose his speech. He discovered that under hypnosis he could diagnose and describe treatments for the physical ailments of others, often without knowing or seeing the person with the ailment. People began to ask him other sorts of questions, and he found himself able to answer these as well.

In 1910 the *New York Times* published a two-page story with pictures about Edgar Cayce's psychic ability as described by a young physician, Wesley Ketchum, to a clinical research society in Boston. From that time on people from all over the country with every conceivable question sought his help.

In addition to his unusual talents, Cayce was a deeply religious man who taught Sunday school all of his adult life and read the entire Bible once for every year that he lived. He always tried to attune himself to God's will by studying the Scriptures and maintaining a rich prayer life, as well as by trying to be of service to those who came seeking help. He used his talents only for helpful purposes. Cayce's simplicity and humility and his commitment to doing good in the world continue to attract people to the story of his life and work and to the far-reaching information he gave.

In this series we hope to provide the reader with insights in the search for understanding and meaning in life. Each book in the series explores its subject from the viewpoint of the Edgar Cayce readings and compares the perspectives of other metaphysical literature and of current scientific thought. The interested reader needs no prior knowledge of the Cayce information. When one of the Edgar Cayce readings is quoted, the identifying number of that reading is included for those who may wish to read the full text. Each volume includes suggestions for further study.

This book, *Dreams: Tonight's Answers for Tomorrow's Questions* by Mark Thurston, Ph.D., covers a subject that Edgar Cayce considered very significant. Not only did he interpret many people's dreams, including his own, but he revealed how to decipher the often obscure messages that our dreams contain. No one is more highly qualified to write on this topic than Dr. Thurston. As Director of Educational Development for the Association for Research and Enlightenment, he has thoroughly researched the Cayce files and lectured widely on the subject. An acknowledged expert, he has written a book that fits Edgar Cayce's basic criteria, that it be helpful and hopeful. I feel sure you will find it to be both.

Charles Thomas Cayce, Ph.D.
President
Association for Research and Enlightenment

Awakening to Your Dreams

You are walking slowly and carefully along an icy road toward a distant destination. It is a cold, crisp day, but bright sunshine glistens in the snow. Just ahead a huge wooden bridge arches over a deep ravine. With great effort you climb up the slippery bridge to its top, and then start down. But now it is the slope of a mountain and you are skiing down with tremendous speed and exhilaration. As you descend, you see something in the sky, just above the tree line ahead. The sky seems to bulge in toward you. Unusual sounds come from the clouds. You are bewildered by their strangeness.

Suddenly, it is as if the sky has burst open—but now all those noises surround you in a different world, and they don't seem strange anymore. You hear the bedside clock ticking . . . a car whisking past the front of your home . . . birds chirping a song to welcome the new day. They are the sounds of your familiar world. It's morning.

You stretch your arms and legs, and then nestle back into your comfortable pillow and the warm spot in your bed. You're in no hurry to get up. Images flood back into your mind again: the bulging sky, the exciting ski run, the icy bridge. How did it all begin? Why were you on that journey? With that simple wondering, it all begins to come back. You remember something about an older woman, but her identity seems to change back and forth between your grand-mother and a favorite schoolteacher of years ago. *She* sent you on that cold journey. You remember the look in her eyes, the urgency, as she gave you the instructions—then you set out.

Now you open your eyes. Fully awake, you sit up in bed. "Better write down that strange experience, before I forget it," you tell your-self. You reach for a pen on the bedside table and scribble down the scenes, the feelings, the story; and you capture the memories of what you have just been through.

You have just recalled a dream—that most mysterious and in-triguing of human experiences, that nocturnal adventure into the in-ner world that has fascinated and bewildered people for thousands of years. Everyone has dreams; yet each dream is so personal and unique that only you can ever fully understand what your dreams mean.

This dream you have just written down is a valuable present. In fact, every dream you have is a precious gift from your own deeper mind.

It may be hard sometimes to see the special worth of a dream, especially if it ends in fear or frustration. But once you learn the se-crets of dream interpretation, you will realize that dreams are your greatest resource for self-understanding, creativity, problem solving, and personal growth.

What are the secrets for deciphering your dreams? Among the confusing array of dream theories, symbol dictionaries, and tech-nique books, there is none better than the approach described in the psychic readings of Edgar Cayce. In more than six hundred readings, his interpretation of about fifteen hundred dreams demonstrates the skill of this psychic source for finding insightful, applicable mean-ings. Anyone who studies these readings is sure to be impressed with Cayce's gift.

Just as important, the Cayce dream interpretation readings con-tain a consistent and effective strategy for approaching dream study. This approach is broad in scope—making room for all the many different types of dreams that an individual may have—and it is learnable. The strategies Cayce used to unveil the meaning of dreams are ones *you* can learn to use today on your own dreams. With practice you may become as skillful as Cayce's own psychic source.

Edgar Cayce would seem to be an improbable figure to be a pioneer in dream psychology. Here is a man whose education barely reached a ninth-grade level. We are more inclined to expect great breakthroughs in dream work to originate with highly trained professional psychologists and psychiatrists. No doubt most of the significant developments have come from such people, but Cayce's contributions are just as important. For example, his material was probably the *first modern source* to document the frequency of psychic dreaming, of diagnostic dreaming about one's own health problems, and of spiritual dreaming, which taps the highest dimensions of the human soul.

We must remember that Cayce's lack of formal education was not the result of some innate lack of intelligence. Family economic pressures kept him from continuing what might have been an excellent academic training in his chosen field: theology and the ministry. Cayce engaged in considerable self-directed study, and he was especially well rooted in the Bible. He also cared deeply about people and was highly sensitive to the needs of others. It should be no surprise that his natural intelligence and compassion spilled over into his trance-work of giving psychic readings. One place where we see this most clearly is in the dream interpretation readings.

Despite the fact that Cayce interpreted about fifteen hundred dreams, relatively few people—twenty-six—asked him for such help. Approximately one thousand of these dream interpretations were given for just four individuals! This may seem to be a weakness in his material, but if we look again we can see it as a great strength of his dream readings. These four extraordinary case histories are available for our study—each with dozens of dreams over many years. In Cayce's interpretations we see the wisdom and the usefulness of dreams to help people through all kinds of life crises. We discover the way in which dreams are reliable friends we can count on, month after month, year after year.

USING THIS BOOK

This book is designed to teach you the approach to dream interpretation found in Cayce's psychic readings. You don't have to be a gifted psychic to make it work. Although there is no single strategy to use on every dream, you can learn a set of techniques that Cayce demonstrated to be productive. Those skills will make you an effective interpreter too.

This book is divided into four parts. Part I offers a foundation for applying Cayce's approach to your dreams. Each of its four chapters is based on the number six. In chapter one you will learn six ways that the Cayce readings define dreams in terms of what they do for you—their functions. In chapter two you will be introduced to six important ingredients to identify in your dreams—their key parts. In chapter three you will examine techniques to improve your recall of dreams—six things to try *before* you go to bed at night and six more things to try *after* you wake up. Finally, in chapter four you will learn the six most important assumptions about dreams on which Cayce's approach is based.

Part II is designed to train you to use the same interpretative skills Cayce used. They are easy-to-learn techniques, and with practice you will quickly start seeing the messages and meanings in your dreams. Many of the examples in Part II come from Cayce's readings, but just as many are from contemporary dreamers.

Part III explores the most exciting aspects of dreaming. We are all psychic at night, and our dreams regularly draw upon extrasensory perception (ESP). This means that sometimes we dream about the future, and other times we communicate with other people in our sleep, perhaps even loved ones who have died. The psychic dimension of dreaming also promises that we can get guidance on specific problems whenever we ask for it. You will learn how you can stimulate this psychic, problem-solving capacity of your dreams. And, even more important, your dreams can teach you that you are a spiritual being. In certain peak, spiritual dreams you may be given an experience of higher realms of consciousness.

Finally, Part IV provides the Cayce Dream Symbol Dictionary, comprising over two hundred symbols that Cayce interpreted in readings. Most of the symbols appeared in several dreams, and so the Cayce readings offered alternative meanings. For virtually every symbol in the dictionary you will find listed other possible interpretations. Remember, Cayce never gave *all* the possible meanings for a particular symbol.

One thing makes this dream dictionary different from any other: the dreams themselves are presented, too. Not only do you see a possible interpretation for a symbol, but you also see the context in which it appeared. For every symbol interpretation given by Cayce, there is a synopsis of the dream in which it appeared. This means that you can use the dream dictionary not only as a handy reference, but also as a learning guide. Here you will discover Cayce's dream interpretation wisdom at work, and pick up valuable clues for sharpening your own skills.

Keep in mind a word of caution about this or *any* symbol dictionary: use it as a tool to get *started*, but never as a "last-word" authority. You will miss too many things about your own dreams and their symbols if you use a dictionary as the sole source of answers. You can begin to add to this dictionary. As you find other possible meanings for a symbol, make a written note of them. You can also compile a list of meanings you discover for other symbols not included in the Cayce Dream Symbol Dictionary.

Now you are ready to get started on Part I. You will see immediately just how practical and understandable the Cayce approach to dream interpretation is. Before long you will be decoding your own dreams with skill and insight—discovering for yourself just how valuable dreams can be. They will help you stay healthy, be more sensitive to other people, overcome obstacles to your growth, and assist you in preparing for your future.

What Is a Dream?

1

The Mysterious Wisdom
of Your Dreams

GORMAN, AT AGE THIRTY-FOUR, was an eight-year veteran of a
big-city police force. He was a tough, street-smart sort of fellow, not
the sort of person anyone would expect to pay attention to his
dreams. But one night he woke up sweating at 4:30 A.M., his heart
pounding. His terrifying dream was still vivid.

He dreamed he had been walking through a rough neighborhood,
on patrol with another police officer. They had received a call about
a robbery and had located the house. Cautiously, they went in. For
several minutes he and his partner moved from room to room, but
the house was apparently abandoned. Gorman turned to enter what
seemed to be a dining room. The room was dark; only a little light
from the house next door came in through the window. He was trying
to find a light switch, when suddenly from behind someone took two
quick steps toward him. As he turned to meet his attacker, he took a
blow to the side of his head and shoulder. Incredible pain filled his
body and he felt a rush of blood from his wounds. Then he awakened
in a panic.

For the rest of the night Gorman slept fitfully. Although he was a
courageous police officer, his dream had shaken him. He was glad
when morning came and he could get up and go to work. He wondered briefly what might have caused that dream. Indigestion from

overeating at suppertime? Watching too many murder mysteries on television? Probably he would never know. And anyway, he wasn't sure he even wanted to know. Activity and routine would help him forget that bizarre experience. But it took several nights before he relaxed enough to sleep well. As the weeks passed, he forgot the frightful dream.

One night he and his partner were dispatched to a house to investigate a complaint of strange events. When they arrived there was no sign of anyone at home, but the front door was wide open. Cautiously, they went in, calling out a warning that they were police officers. Gorman, in the lead, walked down a short hallway. The house was only dimly illuminated from outside lights.

As he peered into the first room, Gorman suddenly recalled his terrifying dream of weeks ago. No logic or analysis was involved. Purely as a reflex he jumped to one side—the vivid memory of his assault in the dream triggered an automatic response. At that moment something whizzed past his shoulder and crashed to the floor. To his horror he turned to see that a man had fallen from the momentum of swinging a deadly ax—an ax that would have landed on Gorman had he not jumped aside. Gorman and his partner quickly subdued and arrested the man. Gorman's frightening dream of weeks ago, by predicting this very event, had saved his life.

TELEPATHIC DREAMING

Alan was a very different sort of person than Gorman, but he too had a remarkable encounter with his dream world. A recent college graduate, just starting his career, he had taken a Saturday morning volunteer job as a leader of a discussion group for teenagers. Here they could talk about the challenges and problems they felt at home, at school, and in relationships.

Of the six or seven youths at each meeting, all participated enthusiastically except one—a fourteen-year-old named Ben. He was a rather quiet and unmotivated boy, somewhat lacking in initiative or self-esteem. Ben mystified Alan and largely frustrated his attempts to be helpful. Although he had been acquainted with Ben's family for several years, he knew of no clear link between his personality and the home situation. Out of concern for Ben, he had begun to pray for him each day.

One night Alan had a remarkable dream. He was walking outdoors and suddenly realized that he was in a dream world. Alan thought to himself, "I want to do something useful in this dream," and he began to look around for someone to help. Ben rode up to him on a bicycle and started to talk. Alan remarked to himself on the clarity of his image—how "real" Ben seemed to be. Ben spoke about why he had a rather withdrawn, unmotivated personality. He described his attitudes toward his own father and some of their difficult experiences together. His father was often highly critical and usually belittled Ben's awkward efforts to do new things. In self-defense, Ben said, he had decided to stop trying. Alan awakened with the strong feeling that he had made a psychic contact with Ben through his dream.

In the weeks that followed Alan's fresh perspective on Ben's behavior in the Saturday morning group made him more tolerant and understanding, less inclined to feel frustrated by the boy's lack of motivation. Finally, Alan decided to verify his dream by calling on Ben's mother. In confidence he told her the dream. She was embarrassed at the family problem and amazed at the accuracy of Alan's dream. The mother confirmed the details of the relationship between Ben and his father. Had Alan's genuine caring for the teenager been the stimulus for the telepathic dream? Whatever its cause, he had gotten a firsthand glimpse of what is possible in the dream state— direct psychic contact with another person.

THE INNER PHYSICIAN IN DREAMS

Kelly, a teacher in her mid-forties, was helped by her dreams to deal with a nagging, worrisome health problem. It had started with an occasional feeling of pressure in her chest. It wasn't painful and lasted only minutes, so she thought nothing of it. As weeks went by the pressure became more pronounced—never really painful, but increasingly uncomfortable. She finally visited her physician. He found nothing amiss but, as a precaution, sent Kelly to the hospital for a stress cardiogram. This comprehensive test proved encouraging: her heart was fine. But the periodic chest discomfort continued.

Soon after, Kelly dreamed she was driving her automobile home and pulled into her driveway. She turned off the ignition key and yet the engine kept running. Greatly dismayed she waited and waited, but the engine wouldn't stop. Kelly got out of the car and opened the hood, although she had no idea what to do next. To her amazement a man walked up to her and identified himself as an auto mechanic. Offering assistance, he removed the air filter and banged it on the ground several times. As soon as he put it back in place the engine stopped running. The dream ended with his pronouncement: "There! That was your problem."

Kelly knew a little bit about dream interpretation, enough to see that this might be a diagnosis of her health problem. She had learned that an automobile is often a symbol for the dreamer's own body. In this dream the mechanic had identified an air intake system as the source of the trouble. *If,* for this particular dream, the automobile represented her body, then there was probably only one good interpretation for the air filter: her respiratory system.

She went back to her physician and asked for a second checkup, this time with special attention to her lungs and bronchial tubes. Sure enough, the condition had now intensified enough that the doctor was able to detect a bronchial inflammation that was the source of her chest discomfort. He gave her the appropriate medication and soon the condition cleared up. But Kelly had made an important discovery for herself: We have an inner physician who has an important contribution to make toward maintaining a healthy body.

GETTING A FRESH LOOK AT YOURSELF

A final story shows another side to the value of dreams. A forty-year-old business manager named Michael was in a tremendous period of change and positive growth for his career. It consumed most of his time and energy, yet yielded big rewards: prestige, a deep feeling of accomplishment, and greater financial independence for his family. Everything seemed to be going wonderfully in his life. Then one morning he woke up after the following dream:

He was on a journey with many other people. They were headed toward Washington, D.C., using all different sorts of transportation. At first he was in a car speeding purposefully toward the destination. Then he became the car itself, feeling the exhilaration of being a high-performance race car—hugging the road with each turn, accelerating through the countryside.

Next he started up a hill; but now it was along a wide sidewalk, and instead of being a car he was jogging through a residential area. He tired somewhat as he neared the top, and glanced at his watch. A boy in a driveway saw him do this and called, "It's 7:15." But the dreamer saw that it was late in the afternoon by his watch—about 5:15. As he rounded a corner, he saw his wife walking up a parallel road on the same hill. She was on the journey too, looking very tired as she carried their small child and led their other child, who looked exhausted. Michael ran over to them. They had *walked* the whole journey. He told her he thought they were near the goal, but she said there was still considerable distance to go. Then the dream ended.

This dream revealed in clear, powerful images how he was taking advantage of his family—putting his career advancement first. He saw *and* felt things that everyone around him probably knew, but to which he had been blind. Now it was suddenly obvious to him.

Two things most clearly struck him from this dream. First was his feeling of remorse when he saw his family so tired and bedraggled. Second was the statement at the end. No, his mad rush for professional success was not nearing its goal. The obsession that was so damaging to the family was not on the verge of achievement—there was still a long way to go. He recognized how the boy in the dream had mistakenly told him that things were further along than they really were (that is, it was really 5:15 and not 7:15).

Michael didn't quit his job, nor stop trying to do his best in his profession. Instead he shifted priorities and adopted a new attitude toward work and family needs. He learned to balance all his activities. That single dream, a turning point in Michael's life, was the stimulus to get his life back on a track that would lead to success in every area.

These remarkable stories provide a powerful demonstration of just how meaningful dreams can be. Skeptics may claim that dreams are merely a residue of our daytime brain activity, or that dreams are just a way for the physical body to readjust itself during sleep—entertaining fantasy with virtually no meaning.

Some dreams, admittedly, are confused jumbles of images and very difficult to interpret. But others are more direct. We all have some dreams that have great meaning, which can help us to meet the problems of daily living in a more creative, productive, joyful way.

Dreams are so elusive and so different from one another that it seems hard to imagine a *definition* for them. But if we look carefully at these nightly events we will also see a way to describe what a dream is. One way is to define what a dream *does* for us. If you think about it, it's often very effective to describe something by explaining its functions. For example, you might be hard pressed to define a locomotive in mechanical engineering terms, but you could easily describe its functions: it travels along a predetermined track, it hauls people and cargo, and so forth.

The Edgar Cayce readings define a dream by showing six functions:

1. Give real experiences in the spiritual world.

2. Provide a symbolic picture of current conditions in our lives.

3. Offer contact with God.

4. Instruct us in a lesson.

5. Present a solution to a problem.

6. Give us a glimpse into the future.

Most dreams exemplify just one or two of these six functions, but occasionally we may have a dream that fits more of them. A good way to see how dreams can help us is to look at some sample dreams in the light of Cayce's definition.

Dreams Are Real Experiences

First, a dream is an actual experience that you have in the spiritual world. Not only is there a physical world of material reality that is obvious to us, there is also a nonmaterial, invisible realm of the soul. According to Cayce, after we die we will continue to be conscious, alive and growing in that nonmaterial world. Each night in our dreams we have experiences that approximate the after-death experience.

The Cayce readings suggest that to a certain extent your dreams are more real than waking experiences. They are likely to show you a deeper reality of yourself, a more authentic encounter with the forces of your mind and soul. These experiences can be so potent that they can make literal changes in you: in the way that you think, feel, and act in waking life. Dreams are far more than meaningless fantasy.

This is not to say that every dream is to be acted out, literally, in waking life. Most often the events of a dream are symbolic. We must develop skills in dream interpretation to see how we can best translate these genuine experiences in the spiritual world into daily physical life.

Furthermore, to say that dreams are real experiences of the soul doesn't mean that a dream is infallible. For example, some dreams appear to be predictions about the future and then don't come true. But even those dreams were most likely a very real depiction of desires or even fears that we had about the future. This first definition of a dream can best be summarized by saying that our dreams are authentic events that happen in a nonmaterial world. Any careful observer will discover just how real they are by seeing that each morning we are somewhat different in attitude and feeling because of the dreams we have just had.

Let's look at a sample dream that illustrates that first function. A thirty-one-year-old man dreamed he was having an argument with his wife and became so upset that he began to beat her. She was knocked unconscious and slowly began to die. The dreamer became remorseful and begged her to come back, promising that their relationship would be better in the future.

Cayce's interpretation suggested that this was an actual experience for the dreamer's soul, designed to make a change in his thoughts and feelings about his wife. Although in waking life he had not beaten her, he had been *neglectful*. The purpose of this dream was to awaken in him feelings of greater care, sympathy, and attentiveness toward his wife. His dream represented a genuine experience of his soul, and it had a profound impact on him.

Dreams Give Us a Symbolic Picture

The second function of a dream, as defined by the Cayce readings, is to give us a picture of current conditions in our waking lives. That picture is from a point of view quite different from the one that we normally adopt in daily living. Here's the way one Cayce reading put it: "In dreams . . . each individual soul . . . reviews or sees from a different attitude those experiences of its own activities" (no. 257–136).* In many of your dreams you are looking at your own life from a new angle, and in so doing you may get important new insights about yourself and others.

This function is illustrated by the dream of a twenty-one-year-old woman: She went into a candy store and asked for ten cents worth of jelly beans. The clerk handed her just four beans. She asked, "Is that all I get for ten cents?" and was told, "Just four." Unsatisfied with what seemed to be an unfair price, she asked, "How much are the chocolates?" and was told, "Three for a dollar." "Just three?" she questioned. She was told again that the price was three for a dollar.

---

*Each of the Edgar Cayce readings has been assigned a two-part number to provide easy reference. Each person who received a reading was given an anonymous number; this is the first half of the two-part number. Since many individuals obtained more than one reading, the second number designates the number of that reading in the series. Reading no. 257–136 was given for a man who was assigned case number 257. This particular reading was the 136th one he obtained from Cayce.

Frustrated, she exclaimed, "Then you can keep your chocolates, too!" and stormed out of the candy store.

This dream occurred in 1925, when a dollar bought ten times more than it does today, and ten cents would have bought a whole bag of jelly beans. Cayce interpreted this as a picture of the conditions in the dreamer's relationship with friends and acquaintances. The prices asked by the candy store clerk were outrageous, and Cayce counseled her that this kind of unfair behavior was exactly the way she was treating other people in her own life. The dream's function was to give her a chance to observe her own unfair behavior from a different angle and to correct it.

Dreams Offer Contact with God

A third function of dreams is to provide an experience that shows how God is working in our lives. Not every dream provides a profound spiritual insight, but you should be alert for this possibility. Here are the words that Cayce used to remind us that contact with God is possible in the dream state: "[Dreams are] a natural experience! It is *not* unnatural! Don't seek for unnatural or supernatural! It is natural—it is nature—it is God's activity! His associations with man, His *desire* to make for man a way for an understanding!" (no. 5754–3).

Many of the interpretations found in the Cayce dream readings told people that they had made an authentic contact with God or the Christ in one of their dreams. One thirty-two-year-old man brought a dream to Cayce in which he had first seen a light, which he knew to be another being. It spoke to him, identifying itself as the Christ. Then the Master himself appeared, in white flowing robes, and took the dreamer on a journey that led to a Palm Beach, Florida, hotel where many wealthy and influential people had gathered. The dreamer spoke and joked with the women gathered at the hotel; and when the Master left and walked out through a gate, the dreamer chose not to follow him but to stay with the women.

Cayce affirmed the validity of the dreamer's contact with the Christ, but he pointed out an important lesson: the dreamer had lost the companionship of the Christ because of the choice he made. Because of his attraction to worldly social life, he lost the spiritual attunement that he had had in the initial part of the dream.

Dreams Can Instruct Us

The fourth function of a dream, as defined by the Cayce readings, is to provide a lesson that is meant to be applied in waking life. This instructive, teaching function of many of our dreams is one of the first things that we will notice as we begin to study them. But the quality of the lesson may vary. Like schoolteachers, some dreams give us better lessons than others. The Cayce readings suggest that the kind and the quality of lessons we receive through the dream state depend largely on two things: the ideals and purposes that we set for our lives, and the extent to which we have applied the lessons that came in previous dreams.

The same man who dreamed of the Christ in Florida brought Edgar Cayce other dreams that provided him with practical lessons. In one dream he told a friend that he was planning to give all of his profits from land investments to charitable causes. In response, the friend criticized and ridiculed him. Then the dreamer's brother appeared and faulted him for having revealed his charitable intentions. The dreamer claimed he couldn't help it, but then he realized that it would have been best if he had said nothing to his friend. Cayce's interpretation was simple: "Don't brag about the good you intend to do."

The same man dreamed that he was in a rowboat. His wife was helping to pull his boat to land. Then he woke up, remembering this short experience. Cayce told him that there was an important lesson about his marriage relationship to be learned from this dream. It was teaching him that his wife had much to offer in the way of assistance, and that he should be more open to receive it from her.

Dreams Can Solve Problems

A fifth function of dreams that is suggested in the Cayce readings is to provide the solutions to our problems. The problem can be very abstract, such as how to solve a difficult mathematical equation; or very practical, such as where to find some old photographs that have been misplaced. Many great inventions and creative ideas have come through dreams. For example, Elias Howe, inventor of the sewing machine, is said to have had a dream that showed him where to place the hole in the needle. Robert Louis Stevenson admitted that one of his best stories was the result of a dream that presented the plot to him.

The key to solving problems through your dreams is to go to sleep with a clear question in your mind. It probably works best if that question is one you have already spent some conscious effort trying to answer.

Many Cayce dream interpretations identified solutions for people. One young woman who had health problems brought him this dream: "It was raining starch and I knew that I should go out in the rain of starch and put it on my side to ease the pain." Cayce found that her solution to a health problem rested with the key word "starch." She needed more starch in her diet. The reading promised relief from a number of physical ailments if she made such a diet change.

Dreams Can Show Us the Future

A final function of dreams is to give us a peek into the future. Although it may sound incredible to someone who hasn't studied his or her dreams on a regular basis, the Cayce readings promise that nothing of any importance happens to us in waking life without our dreaming about it first. Of course, we may not remember that predictive dream, or we may not understand it if it depicts the future in a symbolic way.

When you recognize a predictive dream, keep in mind that the future is not fixed or predetermined. Your dream may forecast a *likely* future event, based upon decisions and influences already set into motion, but it comes as a warning so that you can make changes as needed. Through the use of free will, you can build a different kind of future if that is what you desire.

For example, take this predictive dream of a thirty-year-old man. He dreamed that he was in a field or a woods with his mother and his wife. They discovered a threatening snake and the three of them started running, panic-stricken. The dreamer observed his mother running a zigzag course, and she advised him to do the same. Following her guidance, they all got away safely.

Although Cayce thought the mother in this dream represented the dreamer's real mother, he interpreted the plot of the dream to be symbolic, warning about something that might have caused difficulty for the dreamer in the future. The snake represented those people in his business life who would attempt to harm him in an underhanded manner. The dream predicted that if he followed his mother's guidance and suggestions, he could escape.

All six elements of Cayce's functional definition of dreams can help us develop skills in dream interpretation. Rarely, if ever, do we find a single dream that illustrates all six, and yet many dreams may express two or more. Now that you see these six key ways in which a dream can operate, you are ready to start finding the messages in your *own* dreams.

2

The Anatomy of a Dream

A GOOD WAY TO get started on interpreting your own dreams is to experience the structure of a dream. Think of a dream as a stage play with a setting, a cast of characters, an opening, one or more acts, and a closing. To make this more real to you, let's examine the structure of a typical dream.

We can begin with a sample dream that involves some basic, common elements to which you add your personalized details. The plot and characters of this sample dream may feel familiar to you. Although you may not have had a dream with exactly these elements, many of its images are universally meaningful. At a number of points along the way you can fill in your own details. Just take note of whatever spontaneously comes to mind, no matter how silly. You'll write in the blank spaces your personal images and aspects of the dream story. After you've finished creating your personal version of the sample dream, we'll look at it to identify some of the most important parts of the dream structure—things that we can find in almost every dream.

One way to complete this exercise is merely to *read* the dream script and fill in the blanks with whatever pops into your mind. There are no right or wrong answers. You can learn about the structure of a dream later in this chapter from whatever you do in this exercise.

Your personalized details for some parts of this sample dream will simply make that learning process more interesting.

However, there is another way to complete the exercise, and for most people it is more fun: a dream reverie. This approach requires a friend to help you. First, you and your friend need to be together in a quiet place where you won't be disturbed for at least ten minutes. Get into a very comfortable sitting or lying position. Close your eyes and relax—some slow, deep breathing may help. Take two or three minutes for this relaxation period. Then, when you indicate you are ready, your friend will *read aloud* to you the sample dream script as a guided reverie. Make sure you have instructed your friend to read it slowly, to allow your mind the time to experience clearly each part of the dream story. Some places in the script also require a pause so you can insert your own details for the dream symbols and action. The narrator will find in the script a notation at each pause to indicate how much time is necessary.

Choose whichever method is most appealing to you and experience this guided dream:

A Dream Reverie

It's a beautiful springtime afternoon and you are walking alone down a trail through a hilly forest, full of the sights and sounds of nature. You feel energetic, ready for an adventure.

Just ahead on the trail, you see someone. This person notices you, too, and waves to you to catch up—an invitation to walk together. As you draw closer, you suddenly realize that you know your companion. See now who it is:_____.[*narrator: 10-second pause*]

The two of you walk along together and your companion points out a mountain on the not-too-distant horizon. It must be the tallest one in the area and you feel an immediate urge to climb it—to see what you might find there. Your companion shows you a map, a worn sheet of paper with carefully drawn lines. You're told that it is a secret map, showing a long-forgotten way up the mountain. The map also promises that you will find a guide living in a secluded hut at the base of the mountain.

Soon the two of you find yourselves near the mountain. Using the map, you locate the hidden home of your guide. This guide, who will lead you up the mountain, comes out. To your surprise this person looks familiar. See now who it is:————————————————.

[*narrator: 10-second pause*]

Your guide warns that the journey up the mountain will be difficult and may be somewhat dangerous, but if you follow carefully it will surely be worth the climb. At that moment you realize that on your back you are carrying a pack or knapsack. Inside are three things that may be very useful to the group. You look inside and see these things: ————————, ————————, ————————. [*narrator: 15-second pause*]

Then you start up the trail, your guide leading the way. Your companion is second, and you're behind. The trail is narrow and steep. But all three of you are full of enthusiasm and energy for the climb.

Halfway up the mountain slope you suddenly come upon a huge problem. It is this:

_____

_____

[*narrator: 15-second pause*]

You are bewildered as to what to do. But to your amazement and relief, the guide knows just what to do in order to solve this problem:——

_____

[*narrator: 20-second pause*]

You continue to climb, and before long you all see the top of the mountain. But you see something even more attractive. About a hundred feet below the mountain top you are intrigued by the large opening of a cave. The guide shows you that this is a special cave that is marked on the old map. Inside the cave something of great importance and value is to be found. It will *not* be mere money, but something of even greater significance.

Reaching the entrance, you go in alone. As you walk in deeper, it becomes darker and you must feel your way along, touching the cave's cool, damp walls.

Suddenly, just ahead, you see a brightness. It is a shaft of light streaming down through a natural airhole in the ceiling. It illuminates a spot on the floor ahead of you. And there in front of you is what you have come looking for . . . something of great value and importance for you:————————————————————————

[*narrator: 30-second pause*]

Now your dream begins to fade. The images of the mountain cave start to grow hazy . . . and slowly you regain awareness of your physical body. You are gradually waking up. As you awaken, bring back the clear memory of this dream.

Although this was an imaginary dream, we may be able to interpret it with your symbols and discover something of great meaning. We can also use it as a way to illustrate six ingredients of a dream that are always worth looking for.

THE ANATOMY OF A DREAM

There is an anatomy to a dream, just as there is to the human body. Certainly everyone's body is a little different in shape and size; but there are consistent structures that a physician can depend upon when trying to diagnose ailments or heal a disturbed condition. You can work with your dreams in the same way. As you try to diagnose problems or repair damaged conditions in your life, dreams play a helpful role. Each dream has a reliable structure. Knowing the anatomy of a dream won't by itself give you the interpretation, but it *will* get you started in the right direction. The six ingredients are (1) dream title, (2) opening scene, (3) universal symbology, (4) personal symbology, (5) literal references, and (6) simple story line. Not every dream will have all six ingredients, but you will want to look for all six in each dream you try to interpret.

Dream Title

The first key ingredient to a dream is something that you, the dreamer, can create upon awakening: an overall label, a tag line, or a title for the dream experience. Remember, a dream is like a stage play. Every play has a title, and such titles as *Death of a Salesman* or *The Taming of the Shrew* or *Fiddler on the Roof* are very revealing. They give an insightful clue about the meaning of the entire production.

Take a moment now to review your guided dream reverie and title it. Imagine it is a theatrical production and it needs a title. What words would you pick? Stop now and try this exercise before reading on. Here are some possible titles. Do any of them sound similar to what you would choose? "Journey Up a Mountain," "The Secret Treasure Cave," "Guided to the Top," "Three Explorers and the Mountaintop Cave." Sometimes the dream title you choose is the first important step in interpreting your dream.

Opening Scene

Every dramatic production has an opening scene, and every dream has an opening line. The opening line often provides an important clue as to the meaning of the dream. Take a minute now and look back at the first two or three sentences of the guided dream reverie. What's the opening scene? How would you briefly describe it? Perhaps you would choose words like these: "In a beautiful outdoor setting, I set off on an adventure, walking down a trail."

By itself, this insight does not interpret the dream, but it may give us a clue. It suggests that the dream that follows is going to address some aspect of life that involves a new activity or a new venture of some sort.

Let's look at some *other* dream examples that illustrate the helpfulness of identifying what's happening in the opening scene. One dreamer recorded this experience:

> I'm in an airport. I've completed the first part of my trip, and I'm waiting for another plane to continue the trip. The plane is scheduled to leave at 10:15 A.M. I have plenty of time to make the plane, and I go to the airline waiting area.
> But when 10:15 arrives, there's no plane at the gate. I look at my ticket. It's a different airline, and the plane leaves at 10:20. I'm panicky because I don't know where to find the other airline, and I have almost no time to get there.
> I grab my suitcase, which I notice has new handles, and my garment bag. I leave behind a container of trash that was sitting beside me.

What's the opening scene of this dream play? The dreamer is waiting for a *connecting* flight. She is only part of the way to her final destination. This clue from the opening scene may help her guess that the dream has to do with some part of her life where she is halfway through the completion of some project or life change.

Here's another dream—from the same dreamer—that happened the next night:

> I'm in my backyard, cutting down a tree. I've cut it halfway through and I hesitate to cut it the rest of the way. But I realize the wind might come and blow it over if I don't finish the job.
>
> While I'm getting ready to finish cutting, the tree falls over on its own into the yard. As it falls, it knocks over the brick wall around it, breaking it up into individual bricks. I realize that I want to save the bricks. So I begin to pick up the bricks and stack them in an area of the yard I had prepared for them.

A place to begin interpreting this dream is to look at the opening scene. The dreamer is in her backyard, cutting down a tree. In contrast to a front yard, which is on display for all the neighbors to see, a backyard is her own private space. In the opening line from the dream we also see that she's cutting down or removing something. The dream begins with this kind of opening: I'm in my own private space removing something. The dreamer might expect that what follows in the dream will have to do with some change she's trying to make in her own inner life at the present time.

Universal Symbology

Usually the symbols in your dream are very important in shaping its meaning. But there are different types of symbols. In some of our dreams there are symbols that come from a deep level within us, and since they have the same meaning for all dreamers we call them universal symbols.

The guided reverie dream illustrates two good examples of this. A mountain most often represents a heightened state of awareness. A cave usually represents going deeply into one's own mind—the unconscious mind. Later we will look more carefully at how to interpret symbols, but in this guided dream reverie these universal symbols played a key role in shaping the meaning of the dream.

Personal Symbology

Some symbols are best interpreted with your own associations. Rather than look for a universal meaning, you might ask yourself how certain dream characters or dream symbols may represent your own internal qualities. For example, the person who accompanied you on the mountain climb may symbolize a characteristic within yourself that you most need in order to grow spiritually. Or the specific thing that you found inside the cave might well symbolize a particular talent or strength that is hidden within you. In chapter seven you'll have a chance to learn much more about how to find the meaning of personal symbols.

Literal References

Much of what we experience in a dream is symbolic and represents something other than what it appears to be. Often, however, we dream with a kind of ESP: portions of the dream experience may best be understood in a literal fashion. For example, in your guided dream reverie, take a look at the section dealing with the pack you carried on your back up the mountain. Some or all of the three things you saw in that pack *might* have literal meaning. For example, if you saw a canteen of water it could mean that your body requires more water every day in order to be healthy. If you saw a particular kind of food in the pack it might literally refer to your need for it.

Notice who the person was who accompanied you on this adventure. This might be a person whom you need to be around more often or learn from more directly. Sometimes we dream literally of people and relationships. Certainly, these examples from the dream reverie could also have a symbolic rather than literal meaning. However, it's a good idea always to be on the alert for literal messages. Sometimes the meaning of your dream is given directly, and you can take things at face value.

Simple Story Line

The simple story line is the plot of your dream. Later we will develop the skill of finding the simple story line in any dream. Basically, it involves looking at a dream in its entirety and summarizing in a single sentence the essence of the plot. Often, when we can find the simple story line, we're quickly able to see how that same theme is going on in our waking lives. The entire plot of the mountain-climbing dream reverie might be summarized with these few words: With helpful guidance, I ascend to a hidden place, where I find something of great value. Admittedly, that simple story line misses many of the details. However, it captures the overall pattern of what's going on.

A person who had this particular dream might ask herself, "What ways am I invited by life to ascend to new heights? How can I get in touch with my own inner guide and all of its wisdom and resourcefulness? What kind of a problem along the climb might this dream be warning me about, and what does it show me about a possible solution? What is the reward that is promised me if I am persistent and courageous in this life adventure?" The simple story line gets right to the most important questions raised by the dream. In many ways it's our most powerful tool for dream interpretation.

3

Remembering Your Dreams

How often do you recall a dream? Did you remember one this morning when you woke up? The average person is able to recall only one or two dreams per week. But many people virtually never remember one, and some individuals even doubt that they dream at all.

Nevertheless, clear evidence from sleep laboratories shows that we all dream nightly. Our dream periods come in cycles, typically about ninety minutes apart. Most dreams happen during these times of unusual body and brain behavior called REM—rapid eye movement. The distinctive eye movements beneath closed lids are just one of several characteristics that accompany dream periods. Other features include changes in pulse, blood pressure, and breathing; genital arousal may occur, whether or not the dream has sexual content.

Of course the mind is active all night long, not just during REM periods. Perhaps you've been awakened in the night and noticed that you had been "thinking" about something even though it wasn't actually a dream. In contrast to this ongoing stream of thought, dreams are special experiences that generate vivid imagery, strong emotions, characters, and a story line. These remarkable experiences usually happen about five or six times each night. They range in length from just a few minutes up to thirty minutes or more, with longer dreams more likely near morning.

A DREAM RECALL INVENTORY

What factors most directly influence your dream recall? The ten factors in the questionnaire below may be among the most significant for you. This approach to measuring recall influences, developed by dream researcher Henry Reed, gives you a chance to measure some of the variables that contribute to whether or not you remember your dreams. You must decide how influential each factor is in your own recall habits. Then circle an answer ranging from 0 to 4, with higher numbers meaning greater influence.

For example, Item 1 is, "Waking up at the right moment." Does

Vital influence
Important influence
Moderate influence
Minor influence
No influence

		0	1	2	3	4
1.	Waking up at the right moment	0	1	2	3	4
2.	How much I sincerely expect to remember my dreams	0	1	2	3	4
3.	How emotional the dream is	0	1	2	3	4
4.	Giving myself a bedtime suggestion to remember a dream	0	1	2	3	4
5.	Something the next day reminding me of a dream	0	1	2	3	4
6.	Placing my dream diary by my bed at night	0	1	2	3	4
7.	Being awakened by an alarm clock	0	1	2	3	4
8.	How much morning time I spend trying to remember my dreams	0	1	2	3	4
9.	How colorful, extraordinary, or bizarre my dream is	0	1	2	3	4
10.	How much time I have devoted recently to dream study	0	1	2	3	4

the timing of your awakening make much of a difference in whether or not *you* remember a dream? If it makes little or no difference at all to you, score either a 0 or a 1. If it is a very important factor, score either a 3 or a 4.

Now evaluate each of the ten questions in terms of your own recall patterns.

To score the survey, add the number of points you assigned to items 2, 4, 6, 8, and 10. Next, tally separately the total number of points you gave to the odd-numbered items: 1, 3, 5, 7, and 9.

What do you think these two scores mean? The odd-numbered items, you'll notice, are all rather passive. They involve what happens to you instead of what you make happen. The even-numbered factors cover your own immediate efforts or your inner attitudes toward dreaming. Compare your two scores. If your score for the odd-numbered items is considerably higher, you're probably the kind of person who may hope to remember dreams but sees success as something largely outside of personal control. If your scores are about the same or equal, it shows that the two types of influence have a rather balanced sway on your dream recall. If your score for the even-numbered items is considerably larger, you've probably discovered that success in dream recall is really up to you and can be strongly influenced by your own efforts and choice.

TECHNIQUES TO ENHANCE YOUR RECALL

Virtually everyone who studies his or her dreams discovers that it is possible to increase dream recall. Effective techniques vary from person to person. Here are a dozen possibilities, some of which are likely to work for you, too: (1) review your purposes, (2) go to bed early, (3) read about dreams before going to bed, (4) keep dream-recording materials handy, (5) make a presleep suggestion, (6) learn to wake up in the night, (7) stay in bed a few extra minutes, (8) take a life inventory, (9) relive the dream in reverse, (10) record something in your dream journal, (11) pray or meditate more often, (12) discuss the dreams.

Think of this list as a menu. You may want to experiment with everything on the menu at least once, but only a few items are likely to be your favorites. Later in this chapter you will select four of the techniques to try.

Review Your Purposes

Write down and review regularly a statement of your purpose in wanting to work with dreams. Ask yourself, "Why do I want to remember my dreams and work with them?" At first you may think that this is an unnecessary question, and yet you may have many possible reasons or motivations. Do you hope that dreams will help you change? Do you believe that dreams will teach you something of spiritual reality? Do you plan to have your dreams help you make financial decisions? Each person may have a different purpose.

If you choose this as one of your four techniques in a personal plan to enhance recall, spend at least five or ten minutes thinking about this question. Then write down on a piece of paper your purpose (or purposes) for wanting to remember and work with your dreams. You may also want to review this statement on a monthly basis. People often find that once they start studying their dreams and see more clearly how they work, their sense of purpose begins to change.

Go to Bed Early

Since the most lengthy dreaming periods are most likely to be in the sixth, seventh, and eighth hours of sleep, making sure you get a full night's rest can be crucial to bringing back dreams to conscious remembrance. This technique requires making your dream life a high enough priority for you to forego the pleasures of staying up late.

Bedtime Reading

Read something about dreams just before going to bed. The fifteen to thirty minutes just before you go to bed greatly influences your nighttime experience. You are indirectly giving yourself presleep suggestions by your activities. One way to enhance recall is to take advantage of this psychological fact and carefully select your activity just before going to bed. This might mean reading a few pages from a book about dream interpretation, or it might mean spending several minutes rereading from your dream journal the accounts of dreams from recent nights.

Keep Dream-Recording Materials Handy

Put paper and pencil by your bed. Use a flashlight if your partner would be disturbed if you turned on a light. This enhances recall in two ways: it is a reminder to your unconscious that you're serious about remembering dreams; and it allows you to get some notes written down before it's too late. If you wait ten minutes or more to write down a dream you may find that more and more of the details are rapidly lost. In many ways this is the simplest of dream-enhancement techniques. Another form of handy dream recording is to use a bedside tape recorder. However, you'll probably want to transcribe the recording later in order to have a written account in a dream journal.

Make a Presleep Suggestion

We've already noted how some things serve *indirectly* as sleep suggestions, such as what we read before going to bed. However, a more *direct* approach is to say to yourself silently as you're falling asleep, "I will remember my dreams upon awakening." You might repeat this as many as a dozen times. It is best done in the hypnogogic state, that period of time in which you feel yourself beginning to drift off. It does not have to be the very last thought that you have before falling asleep, but it will work best if done in that state halfway between normal waking awareness and sleep. The thing that makes presleep suggestion work is not the number of repetitions but the *sincerity* of feeling behind the words. As you repeat this suggestion, feel sincerely your desire to remember your dreams.

Learn to Wake Up in the Night

Another technique to enhance recall is to develop a habit of waking up right after a dream. Research suggests that if you don't awaken soon after a dream has concluded, it's unlikely that you'll remember it later. This means that you usually forget most of the dreams that you have in the middle of the night unless you awaken just after they occur.

Of course, no one wants to wake up every ninety minutes. On the other hand, it's possible to train yourself to wake up once during the night, and this awakening will usually take place immediately after a dream's conclusion. Some people have found that this training process is accomplished by drinking a glass of water just before going to bed. It may be inconvenient to have to get up and go to the bathroom at two or three in the morning, but most people have found that after a week or less of using the glass of water, they can stop the water and *still wake up* at the same time at night.

If you ordinarily awaken at least once in the night, try to take advantage of this dream-recall opportunity. Ask yourself upon waking up whether or not you remember any parts of a dream, and then jot down on your bedside notepad whatever you can recall, even just a few key words. It will be tempting, when you awaken in the night having remembered a dream, to say to yourself, "There's no way that I could forget this dream, it's so vivid in my mind." Unfortunately, what's most likely to happen by morning is that the remembrance is gone. All you can recall is that you woke up in the night with some vivid dream that is now lost. However, it's not necessary for most people to write out the dream in total detail when one awakens in the night. Simply getting a *few words* written down on a tablet or paper is usually sufficient to bring back the entire recall the next morning.

Stay in Bed a Few Extra Minutes

This one sounds enjoyable, doesn't it? Many people find that most of their dream recall happens only if they lie in bed in the morning for a short, additional period. Some days you will find that upon first awakening you don't remember anything, and if you jump up and begin the day's activities immediately, no dreams ever come back to mind. However, if you lie quietly in bed for just two or three minutes and minimize any physical movements, you may recover fragments of a dream, or entire dreams may flood back into awareness. You might experiment with this trick upon awakening: lie motionless in bed in your most frequent sleep position. Resuming that posture may help bring back a dream to your awareness—and it can be fun to have a reason to avoid rushing to get out of bed.

Take a Life Inventory

This approach is particularly effective for those mornings when you still don't remember any dreams after lying in bed two or three extra minutes. The life-inventory technique is based on the observation that most people dream frequently about the topics, relationships, and events they think about during the day. Dreams use as symbols the things that have been on your mind in waking life. A simple series of questions in the morning can trigger the recollection of dream events. For example, you might ask: "Did I dream about my wife? . . . about my daughter? . . . about money? . . . about my job? . . ." You can usually complete this mental inventory in about two minutes. Think up about a dozen questions, and then pause for ten seconds after each question to see what comes to mind.

Relive the Dream in Reverse

Often what you will remember at first is only a fragment of the longer dream. If that fragment is only the *ending* (the last thing that happened in the dream as you were awakening), then you must proceed carefully in order to catch more of the dream before it fades away. Resist the temptation to ask yourself, "Now, how did that dream begin?" The orderly side of your mind would no doubt prefer to remember the dream events in a logical time sequence. But when you try to skip from the end of the dream back to its beginning, you may lose it entirely.

Many experienced dream students have found it works best to

relive and recall the dream in *reverse* time sequence. Starting with the ending and moving scene by scene, ask yourself, "What happened just before that?" Sometimes you'll be able to trace the action back through many events or scenes, and you will recall a very lengthy dream.

Always Record Something in Your Dream Journal

What happens if you seem never to remember any dreams in spite of your efforts with these recall techniques? Then try this: write *something* in your dream journal each day, even if it's just how you feel emotionally upon awakening. The value of this method lies in the discipline of paying attention to your own inner states, in this case to your own feelings. It involves committing to paper a description of your inner state upon waking up in the morning.

After several days or weeks of this exercise a person who has had poor or nonexistent dream recall will often begin to remember some dream fragments; or, he or she may wake up remembering just a single symbol that accompanies the feelings. By maintaining the discipline to record simply the feelings or fragments, it is possible to learn eventually how to catch a lengthy dream.

Here's an example of the kind of journal entry such an individual might make using this exercise: "This morning I woke up earlier than usual and felt quite at peace with myself. My thoughts seemed quite naturally to turn to my father, and I seemed to have a positive attitude toward him when compared to my emotions of yesterday."

Become More Involved in Prayer and Meditation

Prayer and meditation are two of Cayce's most frequently recommended techniques for spiritual growth. Prayer is described as an activity of the conscious mind—an outpouring of feelings, thoughts, and words directed toward a spiritual purpose. Meditation is somewhat different. It requires a quieting of the conscious mind so that impressions and inspiration from higher levels of consciousness can be received. Put most simply: prayer is like talking to God; meditation is like listening to God.

The Cayce readings suggest a close relationship between these two spiritual disciplines and dream recall. Something is changed within us as we have regular experiences in waking life with altered states of consciousness such as prayer and meditation. We become more sensitized to other aspects of inner, spiritual life, including dreams. Consistent prayer and meditation is likely to make us more aware of our dreams and increase the probability of recall each morning.

Discuss Dreams with Other People

Get involved with others in the study of dreams. This could take the form of a regular group meeting, or simply talking occasionally with a friend about dreams. Sharing dreams with the family over the breakfast table also works well for many people. The thought and energy you invest in dreams during waking life is bound to stimulate you to remember them more often.

RECALL TECHNIQUES

Look over the list of a dozen strategies for enhancing the frequency and detail of your dream recall. It's probably far too ambitious to try to do them all at once, but you can focus in on just a few now. Pick four items from the list below and make a commitment to work with those four techniques in coming days. Select two from Part A: things to do *before* going to sleep at night or *during* the night. Then pick two from Part B: things to do *after* waking up in the morning. Choose the ones that feel most interesting to you—the ones to which you resonate. Those are the approaches most likely to give you good results.

Part A: What to Do *Before* Going to Sleep or *During* the Night.

———— 1. Write down and review regularly a statement of purpose: Why I want to remember my dreams and work with them.

———— 2. Read or study about dreams before going to sleep.

_____ 3. Put paper and pencil (perhaps a flashlight, too) by your bedside.

_____ 4. Use a presleep suggestion to remember your dreams.

_____ 5. Go to bed early to be sure to get enough sleep.

_____ 6. Train yourself to wake up in the night to catch a dream.

Part B: What to Do *After* Waking up In the Morning.

_____ 7. Lie in bed in the morning, without moving, for two or three minutes.

_____ 8. Take a brief life inventory for subject matter of a dream.

_____ 9. Relive the dream in reverse if all you recall at first is how the dream ended.

_____ 10. Write down something in your dream journal every day, even if it's only how you feel when you wake up.

_____ 11. Get more active with your prayer and meditation life.

_____ 12. Regularly share and listen to dreams with friends or family members.

KEEPING A DREAM JOURNAL

What do you do with the dreams that you do remember? Are they simply stored in your memory? Or do you have them written down on scraps of paper scattered around your house? The best way to work with your dreams is to keep a dream journal. A simple spiral notebook will work just fine, or you may prefer to buy a bound hardback book with blank pages. No matter what it looks like, the key is to make use of it regularly and to discover a format for writing down your dreams that makes sense to you.

You are probably going to want to include several elements in your dream journal. It's a good idea to make some sketchy notes about events of the previous day when you're writing down a dream. You'll also want to date the dream, give it a title, and not only write down the dream itself but any interesting references or ideas that occur to you at that time. It's important to record more than just the dream itself because very often your work of interpreting a dream will happen weeks or maybe months after the dream has taken place. It's often in retrospect that you're able to see most clearly what a dream meant. Making all these additional entries will often be helpful.

Here is a sample of how you might keep a dream journal. This format is only an example, and you should feel free to amend it or adapt it so that it fits you best. No matter what format you decide upon, be sure to start keeping your dream journal tomorrow morning if you are not already doing so. It will give you material with which to work, because in the next chapter you will begin to interpret your own dreams.

Sample Page from a Dream Journal

Notes about preceding day (May 28)

Got up early and had time for some reading and meditation. Worked all morning on refinishing a cabinet. Late lunch. Afternoon shopping. Noticed new problems with car engine. Dinner at Charlie's house. Watched TV until 10 P.M. Read a mystery for an hour before going to bed. Good energy all day.

Dreams during the night of May 28–29

1. I'm driving to the office in a different car—sort of a sports car, red. I seem to be alone, but later there is a passenger in the back seat. Can't see him/her, but I know someone is there. I'm not afraid, but curious. When I stop for gas, I forget to look in the back seat. I'm astonished at the high price for gas at this station.

NOTE: Dream came early in the night—about midnight. Reminds me of a sports car dream of a couple of weeks ago, but in that one I wasn't driving.

INTERPRETATION AND APPLICATION IDEAS:

2. (Fragment) Something about a man who wanted to borrow something from me.

NOTE: The man had features that were a cross between my brother-in-law, who is a policeman, and the clerk at the auto parts store. This was the fragment I woke up with at 6:30 A.M.

INTERPRETATION AND APPLICATION IDEAS:

PART II

Interpreting Your Dreams

4

Getting Started
on Dream Interpretation

Now we're ready to get into the heart of what it means to interpret a dream. Just how do you go about finding the meaning and the help that is available within almost every dream experience? First let's look carefully at what we mean by "interpretation."

Many people hear the phrase "dream interpretation" and assume that means finding the hidden or coded message embedded in the dream experience. This kind of skillful deciphering of symbols is very often exactly what we'll want to do. But we also need to have a broader notion of what interpretation may involve. Sometimes it means just appreciating the experience that the dream has given us—simply recording and honoring the new feelings and attitudes that have been awakened in us simply by having gone through the dream. For other dreams, interpretation may mean taking the message of the dream quite literally. Here it is not so much figuring out hidden meanings behind the symbols but taking the message of the dream at face value. For yet other dreams, interpretation means celebrating the dream: perhaps drawing a picture of it, or composing a poem that recreates its feelings.

The two best-known systems of dream interpretation are those based on the theories of Sigmund Freud and Carl Jung, the European psychiatrists who were pioneers of modern psychoanalysis. Their basic orientations to the study of dreams had fundamental differences.

Freud's approach to dream interpretation involved reversing the process that goes into the creation of the dream. Since the message of the dream, in his opinion, was usually something unacceptable to the conscious mind, it had to be disguised in order to pass through the censor of the ego. This process of disguising the message in symbolic form is called dream work. Hence dream interpretation becomes simply a matter of undoing or unraveling the dream work.

Jung took a different view of the basics of dream interpretation. At the root of his psychological approach was the concept that the human soul is in the process of unfoldment. This process of growth in consciousness could ultimately culminate in what Jung called "individuation." A key principle for our discussion of dream interpretation is that Jung saw the possibility of profound wisdom and insight coming from the unconscious. Frequently a particular level of understanding is available to the unconscious, but is not yet understandable to the conscious mind. For this reason the message or lesson is portrayed in symbols.

Freud thought that dream symbols *disguised* real meaning; Jung believed that symbols *revealed* those same deep meanings. Overall, the approach to dream interpretation demonstrated in the Cayce readings has much more in common with the work of Jung than it does with Freud's work.

PERSONAL RESPONSIBILITY AND APPLICATION: TWO KEYS TO THE CAYCE APPROACH

Before we start practicing specific interpretation techniques, let's make a commitment to two essential features of the Cayce readings approach: *personal responsibility* and *application*.

What does it mean to be responsible for what you learn from your dreams? In terms of spiritual development, we are accountable only for what we know. As our knowledge expands, so does our responsibility to make the best use of that awareness. Anyone who makes a sincere effort to interpret dreams is bound to gain considerable new insight. The key is to take personal responsibility for what you learn and not pass the buck.

For example, a man is having marital difficulties but is unable to determine the root of the problem. He goes to a counselor and together they work on interpreting his dreams. In one session the counselor interprets a dream to mean that the man unconsciously harbors resentments toward his wife for something she did years ago. Assuming that the interpretation is correct, the real test is how the dreamer responds. Will he look to the counselor for the solution to the resentment instead of taking personal responsibility for this needed healing? Will he tell the dream to his wife and expect her to make the changes necessary to mend the relationship? If he follows this course, he is using the dream as a means of an escape. He is escaping from personal responsibility by saying, in effect, "My dream has revealed to me that I am a victim of unconscious conditions controlling my life." Even though this dream has been "interpreted" after a fashion and the dreamer has come to understand himself a bit better, he is not really the better for it.

Just as important, the Cayce readings tell us that dream interpretation really means dream application. You haven't interpreted a dream simply by writing down in your dream journal what you think the dream meant. The real interpretation is putting it into practical experience. Cayce's dream readings always taught that it was in doing something in response to the dream that the real understanding would come. In one dream reading (no. 900–322) he put it this way: ". . . as these lessons as gained from [dreams] are applied in the daily life, there comes the more consciousness of the truths as are shown in same; or in *doing* there comes the understanding."

This kind of application will usually be immediately available to us because for the most part we dream about issues that concern us in waking life. Almost any dream, when properly understood, will have some way of influencing the way you think or act or feel in a practical life situation. It may be a new attitude that your dream encourages you to adopt toward your child; it may be a new way of behaving in relationship to the person next door; it may involve changes in your diet. But if you keep in mind that dreams almost invariably deal with the very same issues that concern you in waking life, it often makes it easier to find an appropriate interpretation.

A PERSONAL INVENTORY

Most dreams are highly practical. They deal with the very issues for which you'd seek advice if you went to a trusted counselor. They comment on the very things you spend the most time thinking about during the day. Let's pursue further this notion that the meaning of your dreams usually relates to some area of your waking life in which you are investing time, energy, or concern.

Use the list below as an inventory of your life. Take a few moments and try to observe yourself. In what parts of your life do you invest the most time and energy? In what parts do you invest the most thought—creative thought or worried, anxious thought? The list below may not seem complete to you, so add items as necessary. Fill in the blanks for relationships with the names of key people in your life now. Then rank each item, using this scale: 3 = a *great deal* of time, energy, or concern; 2 = a *moderate* amount of time, energy, or concern; 1 = a *minimal* amount of time, energy, or concern.

_____ My physical health
_____ My work life
_____ My schooling
_____ My relationship with God or my spiritual quest
_____ Local community affairs
_____ National news events
_____ International news events
_____ The future
_____ My finances
_____ My hobby:_____
_____ My relationship with my spouse
_____ My relationship with my child(ren)

———— My relationship with my parent(s)
———— My relationship with ————————————————————
———— My relationship with ————————————————————
———— My relationship with ————————————————————
———— Other:————————————————————————————
———— Other:————————————————————————————

The source of the Cayce dream readings would probably make this prediction about your dream life: the meanings of most of your dreams relate to the areas of your life you've scored with a 3. That does not necessarily say that at face value you are dreaming about those exact items from the inventory. But once you begin to *interpret* your dreams skillfully, you are likely to find that the hidden meanings and messages from your unconscious mind are commenting directly on these areas of greatest investment. Think of it this way: whatever you "treasure" with your thoughts and concern, there will your heart be also. Dreams represent largely a world of feelings and emotions— a "heart" activity. Hour by hour each day, you are investing energy through your attitudes and emotions. That's the same direction your heart and dream life will take. Of course, your dreams may have a far wiser and insightful view.

Dreams won't just replay your conscious attitudes and under-standings; but the *topics* they address will follow the lead *you* give them. Some of the best examples of this are the interpretations given by Cayce to a young stockbroker who received more Cayce readings than any other person. Morton was in his late twenties and early thirties when he consulted Cayce regularly. His most constant concerns and interests were his stock investments. Not surprisingly, Cayce's dream interpretation often pointed to meanings related to Morton's business dealings.

Here is just one of many such dreams:

I get out of a train at a station and notice that I cannot get aboard again because the doors of the cars are closing. Disappointed and dismayed, I turn for help to a porter, who tells me not to worry—the train would leave, but then pull back in on another track on the other side of the station. Reassured, I go downstairs to cross under to the other platform. But I get lost and miss the train.

Cayce interpreted the dream to mean that in the days ahead railroad stocks would be insecure investments for him. Those stocks would go through many changes and gradually fall off. This example illustrates an important point. Consider this question: If this were *your* dream, would it have had the same meaning? Probably not. Your own associations with trains would have led to a different interpretation for that symbol. The dream might have something to do with your getting left out or left behind. It would have dealt with some issue that concerned your waking life. But for Morton, whose area of constant concern was his stock investments, the "train" image was rather literal.

OTHER BUILDING BLOCKS TO CAYCE'S APPROACH

Dreams originate from a layer of your mind that doesn't operate with familiar rules of logic. No doubt you have noticed that your dreams are often full of contradictions and inconsistencies. Locations switch inexplicably. One dream character transforms into another. People from your childhood and from your current life are mixed into one setting, as if time did not exist. Almost everything about a dream warns you that the usual ways of analysis and order don't work here.

One of the most fascinating implications of this fact is that a single dream can have more than one valid meaning! But don't let that be a source of dismay. Even though you are trying to learn techniques for finding even *one* meaning to a dream, the possibility of multiple meanings doesn't have to make things harder. Instead, it can make dream work more interesting and more fun. This principle suggests that you often have more than one chance to arrive at a useful, applicable interpretation to your dream. But it also says something even more important: Don't stop working with your dream when you arrive at *one* good interpretation. Try *all* the techniques you know until you feel you have found all the helpful meanings. Sometimes you may arrive at only one interpretation, but for other dreams you may find two or three. Most often those multiple meanings will *not* contradict each other, but will be commentaries on different parts of your life. Here's one such example. A forty-two-year-old man brought Cayce this dream:

> My business partner and I are on a crowded streetcar going to a prizefight. The streetcar stops and everyone rushes for the entrance to buy tickets. I race with a mob of people up stairs that look like broken-down terraces. I get to the top first and buy my two tickets. When I open my wallet to pay, I see many checks and bills. But I pull out a foreign check that is essentially worthless. Sitting near the entrance is a woman who has been my bitter enemy for years and who has worked hard and unceasingly against me. But in the dream we greet each other and are the best of friends.

Cayce interpreted his single dream to have two meanings that commented upon two different areas of his life. First, the dream was a warning to avoid bets on prizefights. Note that the symbols related to the prizefight are all rather negative: the mob, the broken terraces, the worthless money. Second, the dream was a prediction about his relationship to the very woman who appeared in the experience. In a few years there is likely to be a reconciliation with that longstanding enemy.

Another key element to Cayce's approach to interpretation is careful attention to *recurrent* dreams. What kind of recurrent dreams do you have? Do they fit one or more of these common themes?

- I'm being chased by an unknown pursuer.
- I'm back in school but unprepared for the exam.
- I'm falling.
- I'm at a party but everybody is ignoring me.

Edgar Cayce himself had a recurrent dream. He told it this way:

> I am walking down a glade with a lady holding my arm. The lady has on a veil so I never do see her face. We come to a brook with very clear

water, beautiful white sand, and pebbles. Stepping over the brook, we start up a hill and are met by a messenger dressed as Mercury. He asks us to join hands, which we do; and then he lays across our united hands a cloth of gold. We walk on up the hill and come to a road that is all muddy. The messenger reappears and tells us to again hold hands with the gold cloth over them; and as we do, the muddy road dries up. We keep climbing—now it's a very high chalk cliff. I have a heavy knife with which I cut niches in the rock. I climb and pull the lady up as I cut. In some versions of the dream I get higher up the cliff than other times. I have never seen over the top and usually I fall.

In a reading given to interpret this recurrent dream, Cayce was told that it occurred whenever changes were coming in his life. The brook represented the dividing line between the old and the new— the messenger symbolizing new thoughts and ideas. The cliff represented the ideals that Cayce strived for. Falling from the cliff was a warning: it was still possible to fail by succumbing to fame, glory, or money. But the interpretation of the veiled, female companion was more vague—that which was necessary to him to be successful in his aspirations. It was required that he stay wedded or joined to those influences in his life. Perhaps the woman stood for his own highest values, or his best talents, or even the support of his wife, Gertrude.

The fact that this was a *recurrent* dream underscored its importance for him. In the same way, any recurrent dream you have probably has special significance. You won't necessarily stop dreaming it just because you decipher its meaning. As long as its message and impact is important to your life, it will probably recur.

A final building block to Cayce's approach to dream study concerns ideals—that elusive realm of values, motivations, purposes, and aspirations. We all have ideals, whether we have stopped to think about them or not. For some people the central motivation in life may be security or notoriety, for others it may be love or service. Whatever your ideals may be, your dreams will regularly comment on them. Dreams will show how you are doing in comparison to what you have chosen as a standard for your life.

Sometimes that comparison is illustrated by a certain symbol that represents your highest values. In Cayce's own recurrent dream, the high cliff was emblematic of his highest motivations. The dream graphically showed him a tendency to slip if he was not careful. In another dream, brought to Cayce by a teenager, the dreamer reported watching a dirigible and an airplane moving through the sky. But the dirigible ran into trouble and crashed to the ground, severely injuring those on board. The interpretation offered by the Cayce reading referred directly to ideals. These flying machines symbolized the high ideals of the teenager's mind. But how are they portrayed in the dream? They crash—the ideals aren't functioning with stability. The dreamer's own lack of strength to follow through on his ideals is pictured for him.

It is not only symbols of height (a mountain, a cliff, an airplane) that characterize ideals. For example, one man presented to Cayce a dream in which he saw a flagpole and the flag flying from it. The interpretation he received was that it depicted the standard by which he judged himself and his actions. The same man on another occasion dreamed he had received a transfusion of his wife's blood—that vital, life-giving force. Cayce in this instance interpreted blood to mean his wife's ideals, which could inspire the dreamer.

However, our values, motives, and purpose are not only *symbolized* in our dreams. In a deeper sense they help shape the very dreaming process. Most dreams serve as a comparison, a measurement, an evaluation of our daily life experience. But that requires something against which to compare. The same principle holds true of any sort of measurement. It's meaningless to weigh a sack of grain unless you have first defined a unit of measurement, like a pound or a kilogram. It's useless to measure the width of a room unless you have first defined a meter or a foot. Our own ideals—which may be spoken or unspoken, clearly stated or only implied by the way we live—play a similar role in dream life.

Cayce's approach to working with dreams is based on certain assumptions. By themselves these features are not really interpretation techniques, but they set the stage for specific strategies. Here again is a set of six key points to keep in mind:

1. You should take personal responsibility for what you learn about yourself in a dream.

2. The real interpretation of a dream is how you apply it.

3. The meaning of your dreams most often relates to areas of your life in which you invest energy and concern.

4. A single dream can have more than one meaning.

5. Recurrent dreams are usually very significant.

6. Your values, purposes, and motives—your ideals—play a major role in shaping your dreams.

5

Finding the Simple Story Line

OF THE MANY INSIGHTS and techniques found in the Cayce readings to help you become an effective dream interpreter, probably none is more important than to identify the simple story line. The simple story line, one of six key features of any dream, is a short restatement of the essential plot. By itself it doesn't interpret the dream, but it is a powerful first step. It serves as a passkey to your dream and can potentially open many doors to greater meaning.

What does a simple story line look like? In the mountain-climbing dream reverie you completed in chapter two, the simple story line could be written this way: "With helpful guidance I ascend to a hidden place, where I find something of great value." Do you see how that catches the essence of the plot, even though it leaves out many details? It gives the fundamental themes and patterns of *what's happening* in the dream experience.

The simple story line is important because it provides an immediate way to tie the dream back to waking life concerns and events. Even though we usually dream about our problems and interests of waking life, the connections may be subtle and not immediately obvious. There are symbols to be interpreted, and so we cannot take everything at face value.

The first impulse of most dream interpreters is to rush to decipher those symbols immediately. They may actually list each symbol of the dream and then start translating them one by one. However, this is often a strategic error. First, you treat the dream in a piecemeal fashion with this approach—you break the dream into parts without first seeing how they fit together and influence each other. Second, the rush to interpret symbols will run headlong into an unavoidable fact: most symbols have more than one possible meaning, even for a single dreamer!

To illustrate this second difficulty, imagine that you have an elaborate dream with many symbols, including that of a *ball*. If you start with symbol interpretation, what will you do with this image? A ball could mean many things to you—a "well-rounded" life, a cooperative spirit ready to "play ball" with others, physical recreation—just to name a few possible meanings. Your efforts to interpret the dream might come down to guessing or following hunches. Even though there is much to be said in favor of following hunches in dream study, you probably want something more than that, some reliable approach that makes it much more likely you will interpret all the symbols correctly.

Here is where the simple story line is helpful. Without actually interpreting, it helps you find the part of your life addressed by the dream. The simple story line of your dream is a statement of its overall pattern. It describes the broad theme of the action and events and treats the dream first *as a whole*. Once you find the simple story line and see how it corresponds to some area of your waking life, then you will be able to interpret the symbols more accurately.

For example, suppose the simple story line of the dream with a ball turns out to be this: Someone who is always a spectator at the game keeps getting accidentally hurt. The next step is to ask yourself where in your waking life this very same pattern fits. Where are you or someone else getting "hurt" even though you are not an active participant? Perhaps you would see that it doesn't fit your relationships at home, nor your opportunities at work. However, suppose that same theme does resemble your own health. You continually have nagging ailments and injuries, and they are probably due to the infrequency of your physical exercise. Even though you enjoy sports, it's principally as a spectator. In this hypothetical situation, the symbol of a ball would represent your need for active recreation. But that symbol interpretation would be possible only because you first looked at the dream as a whole and found the simple story line.

You will need a certain amount of practice to become skillful in identifying the story line. It will be easy for you to see how particular story lines fit the dream examples in this chapter, but you may sometimes feel that you couldn't have come up with that solution if you were working on your own. Two techniques will help you develop this skill and make you more confident: getting into the proper mind-set; and following six specific guidelines. These are (1) focus on action words, (2) use generalizing words, (3) jot down key words and phrases, (4) don't interpret the dream yet, (5) keep it short, and (6) try more than one wording.

The proper mind-set is the one with which you respond when someone asks you, "What's that new movie playing downtown all about?" You may not have time to give all the details, and to tell the complete story would ruin it should your friend decide to see the film. The short summary you give your friend is much like the simple story line of a dream. *It just hits the highlights.* It doesn't try to spell out its hidden meanings, merely what happened.

The short, descriptive blurbs in *T.V. Guide* offer another analogy. They summarize the plot in a single sentence that catches the essence of the story line. The mind-set you would need in order to be such a magazine writer is exactly the same one you'll be using to write the simply story lines of your dreams.

SIX GUIDELINES FOR THE SIMPLE STORY LINE

Focus on Action Words

The most significant aspect of a simple story line is the action. What is happening in the dream? You may want to reread the dream from your journal and underline the important verbs and verb phrases. Here are samples of the kinds of words that are likely to be significant: running away, getting ahead, talking too much, struggling to find, feeling hurried to finish, getting lost in a strange place, and so forth.

Use Generalizing Words

Use nonspecific words like someone, something, things. Many of the nouns of your dream account (that is, the symbols) may stand for something else anyway. So, in the wording of your simple story line, it often works best to use general terms like someone, something, or things. These terms are vague, but they also allow more flexibility when you try to find an aspect of your waking life that matches the simple story line. Here are some sample wordings that use this technique on four different dreams. In each case the general words replace specific dream characters or symbols:

- I unexpectedly find *something* of great value.
- *Someone* underestimates the size of a task.
- I try to get *someone* to help me.
- *Things* keep blocking progress for *someone*.

This part of constructing your simple story line takes the most practice to master. As you become more and more proficient you will start to see different ways to make specific nouns (symbols) flexible and general. You can include key descriptive adjectives. For example, an umbrella in the actual dream may become "something that is protective" in the simple story line. A high wall or a fence in the dream may become "something that limits me." Your grade-school principal may become "someone in authority." In all three of those examples notice how an important characteristic of the symbol is retained, even though the specific person or object is replaced with words like "someone" or "something."

Jot Down Key Words

Usually it's hard to write down the entire simple story line immediately. Your task will be easier if you first jot down significant words and phrases which recall parts of the dream that may be important. This preliminary step allows you to be playful and to look at the dream from different points of view. Most often you end up writing down more words and phrases than you end up using in the completed simple story line. However, by taking the time to give yourself clues and hints, you are much more likely to come up with an accurate and helpful finished product. In some of the examples that follow later in this chapter, you'll see exactly how this process can work.

Don't Interpret the Dream Yet

For some dreams you'll be greatly tempted to formulate a simple story line that goes well beyond the actual dream events and begins to interpret the overall meaning. Resist this temptation. The simple story line technique is limited, but it is very powerful for most dreams. It is designed to help you find a part of your waking life that matches the theme of the dream experience. *Then* you can work with the symbols skillfully to find an interpretation. But if you start trying to write simple story lines that overstep this limitation, the results won't be as accurate.

Think of the simple story line approach as a well-crafted tool, such as a shovel. If it is used for the digging purpose that fits its design, then it will do a good job for you. But if you start using it for tasks it wasn't built to perform—like prying up heavy objects or chipping away stones—the shovel may be damaged and the job won't get done right. Let the simple story line serve you in the way it can do best: to succinctly capture the essence of the dream and help you find a corresponding feature of your waking life.

Keep It Reasonably Short

The most effective simple story line is typically between four and twelve words long. If it gets much longer you are probably trying to put in too much, or you are trying to interpret the dream prematurely.

If the statement you are formulating seems too long, then look back at the dream once again. Does that dream naturally break down into two or three *scenes*? Perhaps each scene has its own short simple story line. Here is an example of a dream that lends itself to two sequential simple story lines, one for each scene in the series of events. The dreamer was a thirty-three-year-old mother of three children.

Dream title: Reclaiming My Baby

I have recently given birth to a son, and even though I've been released from the hospital, he is still there. I go to the hospital nursery and I'm told by a nurse that they cannot find him. She thinks someone else mistakenly took him.

I feel panic-stricken and run outside. A man carrying a baby walks over to me. He says that this is my son. He is very apologetic for the fact that the hospital gave him the wrong child. I look at the child and he doesn't really look like mine. But then he starts sucking his index finger and grabs for my ear, just like I know my son always does. He looks different, but it's definitely my child.

This dream naturally breaks into two scenes: one in the hospital and one outside. Although it is possible to write a single statement for the simple story line, it might be easier and better to write one for each part.

What are the key words and phrases in part one? The basic action is a search to reclaim something that belongs to the dreamer. But what are the most important characteristics of that "something"? It is new (a newborn) and it is precious. The simple story line might be written like this: "I go to reclaim something new and precious to me."

What are the key words and phrases in part two? The most important action is a return and a reunion. But *in what way* does that return take place? With a different and unexpected appearance. And *what* is it that is being returned? That precious, new something that rightfully belongs to the dreamer. So, the simple story line of part two might be written this way: "Something that is mine comes back with a different appearance."

With that two-part simple story line in mind, here is how this particular dreamer proceeded to interpret her dream. When she first awakened from her dream, she was very upset. Naturally, she hoped that this dream didn't warn of some imminent danger to her own young son. But since she was experienced with dream study, she knew not to jump to any conclusions. A baby could symbolize many different things. Perhaps the two-part simple story line would help her find the area of her life addressed by the dream. So she asked herself: "Where in my life am I seeking to reclaim something new and precious to me?" She went through an inventory of various relationships and activities, and found one that immediately fit this thematic pattern.

Three years earlier she had almost singlehandedly organized a nonprofit corporation to aid disadvantaged children in her community. Unfortunately, no appreciable activity resulted, and the organization quietly went dormant. However, in the weeks just before this dream, some new opportunities had begun to arise. People appeared in her life who seemed to want a structure like the one she had created years ago. She had recently been toying with the notion of reactivating her corporation. She had been thinking about reclaiming this "baby."

Supposing for the moment that she had found a promising fit between the simple story line of her dream and an aspect of waking life, she still had to wonder, "What is the dream telling me?" Perhaps the simple story line of part two contained some predictive guidance. It said, "Expect some changes." The "baby" won't look quite the same as it did before; the organization may take on new features as you reclaim it and reactivate it. But if you are sensitive you will notice little characteristics that haven't changed—features that show it has the original identity.

This dream proved to be of profound importance to her in the following weeks. It helped her to keep a flexible point of view as she collected a new board of trustees and officers. Sure enough, the reclaimed corporation had a different appearance than three years earlier, and her open-mindedness allowed it to grow into what it really needed to be.

Try More Than One Wording

Any dream may have more than one way of being viewed. For example, what would happen if you gave to three experienced dream interpreters a copy of the same dream and asked them independently to write a simple story line? You would probably get three different answers. Perhaps there would be similarities, but the three experts might well look at the dream events in widely divergent ways, disagreeing on what parts of the action were most important to the plot.

As you work by yourself on your own dreams, keep in mind the need for flexibility. For some dreams you may find that the first simple story line you compose doesn't lead you to a good interpretation—it doesn't seem to fit any part of your life. In that case go back and try to find another simple story line. See if you can look at the dream action and events from a slightly different point of view. You may have to shift your ideas as to what part of the dream was most important. By the second or third try you should be able to link the pattern of the simple story line to some aspect of your waking life.

THE FORMAT OF A SIMPLE STORY LINE

As you use the six guidelines just described, you will get more and more skilled with this procedure. You'll also probably begin to notice that the great majority of your simple story lines fit one of three formats:

1. Someone [with description] is doing something [with qualifiers] to someone [with description].
2. Someone [with description] is in a certain kind of situation.
3. Things are happening [in a certain way].

Each format has considerable room for creativity in the way that you shape the wording of your thematic statement. Don't let the phrases in brackets throw you. An effective simple story line usually has a few key adjectives and adverbs from the dream. For example, remember the two-part simple story line for the dream entitled "Reclaiming My Baby"? Even though the word "something" replaces the symbol of a baby, the descriptive words "new and precious" are important to include. "I go to reclaim something new and precious to me." That simple story line fits format 1.

The simple story line for the second part of this dream fits format 3. "Something that is mine comes back with a different appearance." Those final four words—"with a different appearance"—describe a certain way in which things are happening. That description is essential to a good simple story line for this dream, and provide the key to its meaning.

Let's look at some other examples and see how they fit one of the three basic formats. Instead of actual dreams we will use well-known fables, parables, and fairy tales. They are "collective dreams" of a culture and we can interpret them much as we would the dream of an individual person—a good start for finding the universal meaning of a fable, parable, or fairy tale is to identify its simple story line.

No doubt you remember the fable about the Tortoise and the Hare. The thematic pattern of this fable's plot fits format 1. Notice the presence of this structure: Someone is doing something to somebody. The simple story line might be worded something like this: "Someone slow but steady outraces someone fast and over-confident."

Or recall the story of the Three Little Pigs. The big, bad wolf is able to blow down the houses built of straw and sticks, but is powerless against the house of bricks. The simple story line here fits format 2: Someone is in a certain kind of situation. For the first half of the story we might capture the essence of the plot with these words: "Two who are lazy fall prey to destruction." On the other hand, the plot switches in the second half of the story. Words such as these convey the simple story line: "Someone who is conscientious and works hard is secure."

Sometimes a fable or story can be seen from two perspectives, and so two different kinds of simple story lines emerge. For example, think for a moment about the story of Noah's Ark. If you view the narrative impersonally, then format 3 works best: "Universal inundation destroys all but a chosen few." However, if you see the story principally in terms of Noah and his activities, then format 1 is more appropriate: "A good man who follows divine guidance saves a chosen few."

What might you create as a simple story line for the tale of Goldilocks and the Three Bears? It often helps to jot down key words and phrases first. Your list might include *wandering girl, vacant house, enters uninvited, makes herself at home,* and so forth. Format 2 seems to be most promising because the story revolves around how Goldilocks gets herself into an embarrassing situation. Perhaps your final wording would be, "Someone who is wandering and uninvited gets caught making herself at home."

What about the fairy tale Cinderella? Again, the story line you create depends on the point of view from which you see the plot. If you focus on the forces at work in the story, then format 3 will work best. The simple story line could be, "Good-hearted sincerity plus magic change a poor girl into a princess." On the other hand, if you see things primarily from the standpoint of the situation into which Cinderella is placed, then format 2 is more appropriate. In that case the simple story line might be, "Someone overworked and unappreciated gets magical help and marries into royalty."

As a final example, consider Jesus' parable of the Prodigal Son. Format 1 is probably the best candidate. Before you try to write out a wording for the simple story line, here are key phrases you might list: *tolerance, wasting of money, change of heart, return, welcoming home, forgiving parent.* You could try to arrange the items on that list to fit the structure of "someone does something to somebody." It might come out looking like this: "Someone tolerant and forgiving welcomes home someone wasteful of resources."

These examples merely illustrate the technique. Fables, parables, and fairy tales aren't exactly like your personal dreams—they contain more universal symbols than most dreams. Nevertheless, because they are so widely known and recognized, it can be fun to find simple story lines for them. It's a good way to practice the skill.

EDGAR CAYCE AND THE SIMPLE STORY LINE

The Edgar Cayce readings often used the simple story line to interpret dreams for people. For example, one man brought this dream to Edgar Cayce:

I go to play golf with my wife and a business associate. My two companions make their opening tee shots and only then do I discover that I have left my golf clubs in the locker room and have to go back after them. I realize that it will be too late by the time I get back with my clubs. My companions are going to have to go ahead without me. They can't hold up all the other people waiting to start just because of me. I am unhappy about this because I'm not comfortable with having my wife playing golf alone with this person.

In interpreting this dream, the Cayce readings went right to the simple story line. It might best be worded this way: "Things go wrong because I'm not prepared." This one fits format 3. The Cayce reading was able to show the dreamer how this very theme was quite relevant to a number of conditions in his waking life.

On another occasion the same man brought Cayce this unusual dream, in which the simple story line was actually stated by the dreamer at the end of his account:

I am in the office of my deceased father in the city on a Sunday morning. The office building is empty except for a watchman. I am in the office, anxious that I might be discovered. I squirt a small amount of liquid into my eye with a syringe. Then the watchman finds me and punishes me by squirting my eye full of water with a hose. He gave me plenty of that which I sought in secret to have in a small quantity.

The interpretation focused on that closing summary, emphasizing the essence of plot given by the simple story line. Cayce linked the simple story line to the man's search for greater spiritual knowledge. The dreamer was warned about being blind to full understanding if he tried to seek by private, secretive methods. To search for truth in a reclusive way—in small squirts of liquid—would never wash clean his spiritual vision. Instead he needed two things: to receive a full quantity of truth; and to adopt an attitude that spiritual life is not secretive but practical and applicable—open for all to see.

In another instance Cayce used the simple story line to interpret the dream of a twenty-three-year-old woman. She saw herself driving a new car away from a restaurant with her husband. As she drove along a lakeside road, all at once she went up over the embankment. The car stopped, tottering on the edge, about to fall in the lake. The dreamer thought to herself that she could jam on the emergency brake. It would have held the car long enough for them to escape unhurt. But she didn't do it. Instead she jumped out of the car into the lake. The car then fell into the lake on top of her and killed her.

Cayce's interpretation pointed to a simple story line that might be worded like this: "I fail to do what I know would keep me and someone else safe." He then related that theme to her tendency in life not to follow through on things she knew she ought to do. The dream graphically illustrated the self-destructive results of such negligence.

In yet another instance Cayce again used the simple story line to interpret the dream of a different young woman. She sees herself in a situation where she is expected to marry her cousin William. But she "hems and haws" and hesitates, delaying any decision about the marriage.

Cayce's interpretation had nothing to do with her relationship to William nor to literal marriage with anyone. He first identified a simple story line: "I am hesitant to make commitments." Next he described how that fundamental tendency was present in several parts of her life.

QUIZZING YOURSELF ON THE SIMPLE STORY LINE

Now try your hand at finding a simple story line, keeping in mind the six guidelines:

1. Focus on the action words.
2. Use generalizing words, such as someone, something, things.
3. Start by jotting down key words and phrases.
4. Don't interpret the dream yet.
5. Keep it reasonably short—four to twelve words.
6. Try more than one wording when needed.

Your quiz to practice this skill covers two famous stories and three sample dreams. Right after the final dream, you will find suggested wordings for good answers. But try to come up with your *own* simple story line for each one of the five *before* you look at those suggested wordings.

- Story 1:   The biblical account of David and Goliath.
- Story 2:   Jesus' parable of the Good Samaritan.
- Dream 1:   I am in a hurry to get someplace, and so I speed in my automobile. I notice that my car license number is being written down. Soon thereafter I am stopped by a policeman, which greatly delays me.
- Dream 2:   I go to a gymnasium to play basketball. A lot of other men are there wanting to play, too. Someone determines that only those who are already professional basketball players will be allowed to play now. There are eight people, including me, who qualify. I sense that many of the others are angry or disappointed at being left out. I suspect that some of this emotion is directed at me, because I'm shorter than some of those who won't be able to play. But I realize that I am a member of a professional team and I insist on my privilege to play.
- Dream 3:   I watch as an airplane soars up into the sky, trying for height and height alone. Unexpectedly, it comes to a sudden and disastrous stop. It plummets to the earth, leaving a wave of flame from its fire.

More than one good solution is possible for each story and dream. You need not feel that your wordings for simple story lines must exactly fit those given below. You may find several equally promising points of view to take in summarizing the dream plot. As an example, however, here are the simple story lines that might work well for each of the five items in the quiz.

Story 1

The story of David and Goliath nicely fits format 1: someone is doing something to someone. Does your wording look something like this good answer? "Someone small, confident, and resourceful defeats someone big and intimidating."

Story 2

Jesus' parable of the Good Samaritan could fit either format 1 or 2. If you chose format 1, perhaps your answer looks like this: "Compassionate traveler provides unexpected help to someone in need." Or, if you used format 2, your answer may be like this: "Someone who is hurt gets support from an unexpected source."

Dream 1

The first dream is taken from the Cayce readings. A young man brought this account to Cayce and the reading interpreted it by focusing on the simple story line. Format 3 is probably most appropriate in this instance, although you may have seen a way to describe the essential plot with one of the two other formats. Does your wording look something like this? "Trying to rush results in a big delay." Cayce pointed out how his tendency to rush things in waking life would backfire and only take up even more of his time.

Dream 2

The second dream was one of a contemporary man. Here are some of the possible good wordings for the simple story line: "Despite shortcomings by appearance, I claim the place for which I am qualified." Another possibility would be, "People are envious of my privilege." A third good answer would be, "Others disapprove, but I know my talent qualifies me for a special opportunity." Your answer may not be in these exact words, but does it seem to point in the same direction?

The context for this dream was this: the young man had recently been hired for a job, even though he lacked certain experiences that other applicants had. In his conscious life he questioned whether or not he really deserved this excellent job opportunity. The dream illustrated his dilemma. Using the simple story line, he was able to see clearly that despite whatever shortcomings may appear on the surface, other people's jealousy or disapproval was unwarranted.

Dream 3

The third dream was another brought to Edgar Cayce. Cayce's interpretation focused on seeing how the simple story line fit what was happening in the dreamer's waking life. Here are some possible wordings for that simple story line: "Something climbs too high, only to end up in destruction." Another possibility would be, "Concern only for height leads to disaster." A third possibility would be, "A sudden unexpected fall results in destruction." Edgar Cayce's interpretation was that the dream warned how a desire for fame and notoriety, especially through the development of psychic ability, would only lead to a sad conclusion.

Now that you have practiced on famous stories and the dreams of other people, you can turn to some of your *own* dreams. Pick two or three of your recent dreams and write a simple story line for each one. Does it match a part of your waking life? If the fit doesn't seem to be obvious at first, don't despair. The next chapter presents five effective ways to discover how the simple story line matches daily life concerns.

6

How the Dream
Fits Your Life

IMAGINE THAT YOUR LIFE is like a complex jigsaw puzzle that you
are trying to put together. It is composed of hundreds of colorful
pieces, each with a unique shape and appearance. Every event in
waking life is a piece of this puzzle, and so is every dream. As you fit
together more and more of the pieces you begin to see the big picture
of who you are and what the meaning of your life is.

Suppose your jigsaw puzzle is about half-assembled, and now you
have in hand a piece that represents last night's dream. Where does it
go? How does it fit in and add to your overall understanding?

To find the correct position for this puzzle piece—this dream
from last night—you may want to use the simple story line technique.
Ask yourself, What is its overall pattern and appearance? How would
you describe it? For example, is it a greenish, elongated piece with a
square end? Or is it a speckled white and blue piece with four sym-
metrical nobs?

Sometimes you cannot see where it goes, even when you have
described the overall pattern. You need a clue as to where it fits in the
overall puzzle. For example, you might try it somewhere near the
bottom left-hand corner, or use it to start a new section in the upper
center. In the same way useful hints can help you match your dream
to the other patterns of your waking life. You may immediately see

how your dream fits, and you won't need these strategies. But often you'll need some extra assistance from the five approaches described in this chapter: (1) problem-presentation dreams, (2) compensatory dreams, (3) physical health dreams, (4) desire- and fear-produced dreams, and (5) dreams with a play on words. *Sometimes these techniques work in conjunction with the simple story line. Other times they help you find the message of the dream when the simple story line approach wasn't successful.* Let's look at these techniques one by one.

PROBLEM-PRESENTATION DREAMS

Take a closer look at the simple story line of your dream. Does it revolve around a problem or difficulty? Does it involve an unresolved conflict? Does your dream contain an adversary—a person, an animal, or even the elements of nature? It may be you, the dreamer, who faces the problem, or it may be another dream character. You may find the following kinds of words in its simple story line: unfamiliar, unpleasant, unsuccessful, darkness, obstacles, terrifying, intimidating, panic, tormenting, despair, frustration, futility, rejection, distress, disappointment, victims, irritation, inadequacies, assailants, restraints.

However, just knowing that the dream presents a problem isn't enough. To *which* problem from waking life does it correspond? In order to find exactly where in your waking life this dream fits, begin by asking yourself questions that begin *what, who, why, when, where.* They probably won't all be helpful, but one or more may stimulate an insight about your problem-presentation dream:

- *What* is the problem in the dream?
- *Who* is having the problem?
- *What* is shown in the dream as the cause of the problem?
- *Why* did it happen?
- *What* is the reaction of the person who faces the problem?

- *What* mistake is he or she making?
- *What* is the first step to finding a solution?
- *Whom* can the person go to for help?
- *When* is the best time to act?
- *Where* would be the place to begin?

First, these lines of questioning help you to see how the dream fits with your waking life. Second, they may help you to see a guidance message about how to deal with the problem. You may be able to infer a solution to your problem by the way it is presented in the dream. Even though the solution itself may not be given in the dream, you still may be able to formulate one because of what you see in the dream. Let's look at two examples that illustrate how this can work.

Molly's Dream

Molly, a forty-three-year-old research scientist, was part of a university team that was lookng for funding to support new projects. They had several possible sources, yet negotiations were slow and difficult. Molly thought it might be quicker and less frustrating to do it on her own, so she was entertaining notions of trying to get her own funding. Then she had this dream, which she later entitled "Going Down the Wrong Road."

> I am with a group of people traveling in a large vehicle down an interstate highway toward some destination. Things shift and we are all in our own individual vehicles, traveling in caravan on the highway. But I become impatient and pull into a different lane, trying to get out to lead our group at a faster pace.
>
> A large, slow-moving truck is in my new lane and keeps me at the same slow speed. But what is worse, I suddenly realize that the highway has just forked. All my companions were in the lane that veered off to the left and merged with a different highway. At first there seems to be no way to rejoin them, and I don't even remember what their cars look like.
>
> Then, to my surprise, I see just ahead one final chance to get over onto the different highway. It's a small, unmarked exit, and it requires

the greatest of care because it involves yielding and making a turn across oncoming traffic. As I prepare to make that careful turn I see on the different highway the last of my companions headed down the road. Perhaps I can still catch up with the group again.

The opening scene of the dream—like the opening scene in a dramatic play—provides the first clue: she is headed toward something with other people. Next Molly formulated this wording for the simple story line: "I get cut off from others by impatiently following my own path."

Clearly, this is a problem-presentation dream. She was quickly able to see how it fit her situation at work. But does the dream go further than just restating her frustrations? Can she infer a guidance message from the dream? Molly concentrated on two questions that helped her to see the best steps to take in her professional life. She asked herself: "What mistake am I making? When is the best time to act?"

She made the erroneous assumption that things would proceed more efficiently if she stepped out and asserted a leadership role. Not only did she have a mistaken notion of the proper timing, but also of the correct lane or pathway. When is the best time for her to *act* on a solution to the problem? Immediately. She is given an unexpected opportunity to get back with her companions, but it will require utmost care and no hesitation. Otherwise, the group will soon be out of sight.

Elizabeth's Dream

The story of Elizabeth, a thirty-three-year-old executive secretary and mother, also illustrates how the simple story line of a dream can describe a problem in life. One night she had the following dream, which she later entitled "Unequipped for Skiing."

I am on a hill covered in snow, with two men. I don't recognize them, but at the same time I feel that I know them. We are looking down the hill, contemplating the route to ski. The way is steep and I am about to proceed down when I realize that I don't have any ski poles. I'm not quite sure how I am going to maneuver the hill without the poles. I know I am good, but I am not an expert skier.

The opening line of the dream gave a first clue to its meaning. She found herself in a challenging situation. The two men could have symbolized specific men in her life, or they could have represented masculine aspects of herself. As she began to interpret the dream she couldn't yet be sure. Her next step was to write a simple story line: "I don't have the right equipment I need to handle a situation in the best manner."

The simple story line summarized her dilemma in the dream. It was clearly a problem-presentation dream, but what waking life problem did it match? As she carefully reviewed recent events in her life, she found an answer. The previous day she had had a run-in with two friends. Something she said had hurt their feelings, and she had been surprised by their strong reactions. These familar people were suddenly strangers to her, showing sides of themselves she had never known. She had gone to bed that night still worried and uncomfortable about the problem.

The dream had symbolically portrayed her difficulty. She wasn't equipped with the interpersonal skills to deal with this challenge, so it was best to back off and not push the issue for the time being. Perhaps later she would have what she needed to "ski down this steep mountain" and to resolve tensions in the relationships.

Ted's Dreams

A final example of problem-presentation dreams shows another significant feature: a *series* of dreams with a common simple story line or problem. Ted was a forty-six-year-old business executive who had become bored and restless in his profession. As he toyed with the notion of changing careers he had a series of three dreams in one week. Here is his first dream:

I have just qualified to be a professional golfer. I am at my first tournament, about to tee off as the fourth player in my group. But when it is my turn, I never seem to be able to get around to hitting the ball.

There is always some little thing wrong—someone is in my way, a tuft of grass is not sitting right, my swing is obstructed by a spectator. My three playing companions have finished the first hole and moved on to the second. I am left still trying to get off my first shot.

What a graphic depiction of his waking-life career problem! The dream gave Ted a first clue about how to resolve it. He needed to be aware of his tendency to hesitate before acting—to insist on everything being just right before getting started.
Here is his second dream:

I am watching two physicians interact. The older man is a highly respected obstetrician. The younger man has just finished medical school and is starting his residency work. The young doctor aspires to be part of the team headed by the older physician, and has confided this great hope in a few friends. But one friend misunderstands him to have said that he *already* works for this older doctor. Rumors get around and the older doctor hears about this false "claim." He is outraged at the young doctor's audacity to tell people such a lie. Apparently, the young doctor has lost his chance ever to fulfill his aspiration.

Clearly, this dream presented Ted with a problem. The simple story line that he wrote in his dream journal said, "Someone talks about plans and it leads to missed opportunities." Amazingly, another dream four nights later presented a similar problem and simple story line:

I am sitting in a restaurant with many people and strike up a conversation with a married couple sitting next to me. The woman announces that she has just written a new country and western song. She sings some of it for everyone in the restaurant. It is obviously very good and sure to be a commercial success. But then I become very concerned that the woman has made a big mistake: she has jeopardized her project by having revealed publicly the tune and words of her song.

Here again Ted has dreamed of a situation in which public disclosure undermines the likelihood of success in the future. The message seems clear: the best way for Ted to deal with his career problem is to keep quiet about new plans he is formulating.

COMPENSATORY DREAMS

Compensastory dreams try to create balance in your life. Carl Jung, a pioneer of modern spiritual psychology, is best known for this technique of dream interpretation, but it is also found in Cayce's dream readings. One Cayce reading (no. 1968–10) states, "Oft [dreams] may be as opposite that which is presented to the body."

The method is based on this principle: the human mind ever seeks balance and equilibrium. For example, whenever you go to an extreme in your waking life, your unconscious mind will produce the opposite extreme to reestablish a balance. Since dreams come from the unconscious, you might well expect that many of those nighttime experiences are compensating for extremes during the day: extremes of attitude, emotion, or behavior.

The classic example of this process is a dream in which you are embarrassed to find yourself naked in a public place. Almost everyone has had some version of this simple story line in a dream. But what does it mean? There are many possibilities, but often such a dream is compensatory. To see how this is so, ask yourself, "What is the opposite of being exposed to many people?" No doubt you'll see that the answer is something like this: "to be covered up and hidden from people." The dream of nakedness may serve the purpose of creating a balance within your mind. Such a dream is *not* guidance to strip off your clothing in public, it is a reminder to find the middle ground between extremes.

One man brought a dream to Edgar Cayce that proved to be compensatory.

> I am at my job on the New York Stock Exchange. I am interacting with my colleagues in a joking, smart-aleck fashion. I feel badly for acting this way.

Although the interpretation given in the Cayce reading doesn't define the simple story line, we can come up with one. It might be this: "At work I behave in an extremely light-hearted way." Cayce's interpretation began with the assertion that this dream should "be considered or treated as diagonal, or in the opposite from conditions" (no. 137–76).

What is an opposite of the simple story line here? Certainly there is an extreme, but what is the counterbalancing extreme? Behavior that is staid, overly serious, and old-fashioned. This was exactly how the Cayce reading said the dreamer was acting in waking life at his job. But what, then, is the meaning of the dream? To become a smart aleck in his profession? No, it is to find a balance between the two extremes.

Michael's Dream

A final example of this process involves a contemporary dreamer—Michael, a twenty-five-year-old graduate student. In the weeks just before this dream his life had become more and more unstructured. More and more his approach to life affirmed, "Just go with the flow." Although he seemed to be perfectly satisfied with this attitude, something deeper within him apparently wasn't. Here is his dream:

> I am at some public place like a park. It has many exhibit buildings and I want to go inside one. Coming out of it is a whole company of uniformed military men. I realize that I too am in the army and in uniform. As I pass each one of them, I salute. I hope that I have done it right, because I am new to the army. Then a friend stops me to admire my appearance in uniform. I think to myself that the army is not so bad after all. It is teaching me about some of the realities of life.

There are several good possibilities for the simple story line, but one could be: "I take pleasure in my new, regimented life." One approach to fit this simple story line to his waking life would be to look for a compensatory opposite. His reflection could be worded, "I take great pleasure in my *undisciplined, unstructured* life." In fact, this opposite extreme was exactly what was going on in his waking life. The dream was a call to find greater balance between spontaneity and regimentation.

PHYSICAL HEALTH DREAMS

One of the greatest contributions of Edgar Cayce's readings to our understanding of dreams concerns physical health. Time and again his readings showed people how their dreams were providing diagnostic and prescriptive guidance. We are shown that on a regular basis our *own* dreams give us a "physical health reading."

Cayce suggested that nightmares are often caused by physical instability, such as incoordination of the sensory-motor and autonomic nervous systems, or imbalance in the digestive system. These physically produced dreams are not only the scary type of dreams we usually call nightmares; they may also be bizarre, jumbled dreams that lack any sort of story line.

Of greater interest is a physical dream that diagnoses an ailment, warns about an impending health crisis, or recommends specific procedures for healing. One way to fit the simple story line to your waking life is to look for just that sort of dream message. There are many instances of this process in the Edgar Cayce readings. Let's look at two dreams from a twenty-two-year-old woman.

> My husband and I are watching a series of automobile accidents in which many children are killed. Then we move on, and pay no more attention to this. We enter a candy store. My husband wants to buy candy, but I warn him he shouldn't do that.

Edgar Cayce's reading indicated that the simple story line fit conditions of her own health. If we were to take her dream now and try to write a simple story line we might find it best to write separate ones for each of the two scenes. Part one has this theme: "We watch physical harm and even death come to some people." Part two then has this theme: "Someone indulges in food he really shouldn't eat." It seems reasonable to conclude that this relates to her own dietary patterns and contains a serious warning. In this instance the reading suggested that the dream was relevant to both the husband and herself.

Here's her second dream:

> I am standing on a rickety old platform beside a pond. I dive head first into the pond, doing a belly-whopper that hurts my stomach.

We might word the simple story line of this dream like this: "I jump into something from a shaky foundation and get hurt." The reading interpreted it as a physical health dream and warned her not to jump into pregnancy while her body was still in a shaky, unhealthy condition. Cayce's reading cautioned her that she would likely miscarry the child if she became pregnant soon. In fact, the woman later got pregnant and soon after had a miscarriage.

How might the dreamer have recognized this to be a physical health dream? She might have looked for a clue: Does a part of the body play a key role in the dream story? Yes, her belly does. This clue might have tipped her off to the dream's message. This is *not* a hard-and-fast rule, but it often provides a good way to recognize health dreams.

The setting of the dream can also indicate a health dream. Henry was in the midst of a two-week-old head cold, and the runny nose and coughing were really getting him down. No remedy seemed to help. Then he had this dream:

> I am on a journey by foot, hoping that a motorist will pick me up. I find myself walking through a small town. Along the sidewalk I am harassed by three men of tall stature and great strength. To avoid them I duck into a restaurant and its men's room. But when I come out, one of them is waiting for me. He says the leader of the three is irritated with me because I am a vegetarian.

Both the restaurant setting and the dietary reference tipped him off to the likelihood that this was a physical health dream. Henry didn't feel that the message was to give up his vegetarian diet; yet it clearly appeared to deal with his health and his difficulty in getting over the head cold. When he took time to review his diet, he saw that he had been relying almost exclusively on dairy products for his protein. He now guessed that these mucous-producing foods were contributing to his problem. He shifted to alternative sources of vegetarian protein, and began to see improvements in his health almost immediately.

What other settings can be clues to physical health dreams? A bathroom (such as the men's room in Henry's dream) often symbolizes cleansing for the body. A kitchen or dining room frequently represents dietary issues. A health-care facility—such as a clinic, hospital, or doctor's office—is often the setting for a dream about one's physical health. A drugstore may literally refer to drugs and their effects, such as in the following example, which a man in his late twenties brought to Edgar Cayce:

> My brother and I try to find a drugstore at night in Brooklyn. We get lost in a tough, dangerous neighborhood, and threatening people are lurking about. When we find the drugstore, its entrance is blocked by a menacing character.

Not surprisingly, Cayce interpreted this dream to be about physical health. The reading stated directly that this was "warnings as respecting the relations of self as regarding drugs" (no. 900–322). Even if the young man had not had Cayce to interpret this dream for him, two factors should have shown him its message: (1) a simple story line that would include the theme of threat and danger; and (2) the setting near a drugstore.

DESIRE- AND FEAR-PRODUCED DREAMS

Not every dream that looks like a warning is necessarily a prediction of impending trouble. Not every dream that shows you doing something new or different is guidance that you ought to do it. A very important approach for interpreting your own dreams is to be alert for desire- and fear-produced dreams. Learning to recognize them can save you considerable misunderstanding.

Let's consider first of all how your dreams may be created. In Edgar Cayce's theory of the unconscious mind, dreams reflect an intuitive kind of reasoning and comparing by the deeper levels of the mind. This creativity is directed by the wiser will of the soul, which seeks spiritual growth and development. But Cayce's readings mention another method by which some dreams can be produced. Desires *or* fears from waking life may force themselves onto the dream world. The dream you then wake up remembering is not guidance from your own higher self, but a depiction of those desire patterns or fears.

Desire-Produced Dreams

Freud called desire dreams "wish-fulfillment" dreams. Sometimes we may not be fully conscious of just how strong our desire patterns really are. Maria's story shows just how much needless trouble can happen to a dreamer who isn't aware of this approach to dream interpretation.

Maria, a woman in her early thirties, very much wanted to get married but simply hadn't found a man who met her high standards. One day, to her delight, she met a new employee at the company where she worked—a man to whom she took an immediate liking. In virtually every way, he had the qualities she was looking for. Not only that, they seemed to hit it off right from the beginning. She wasn't able to tell if he was interested in a romance, but she certainly was.

She soon began to dream about this man. In every dream she was either married to him or about to get married. She quickly and willingly interpreted her dreams to be guidance from God that this man was meant for her. But, to her dismay the months that followed were full of frustration and emotional pain. As she tried her best to pursue the relationship, she discovered that he was interested only in being friends at the office.

Maria was embarrassed by her failed overtures and angry that her dreams had tricked her. What she failed to realize was that this series of apparent guidance dreams had really been produced by her own desires. They weren't guidance from a higher source. So much of her distress could have been averted if only she had paused and ask herself: "*Does this dream merely show something that I desire?*"

Fear-Produced Dreams

The same kind of process can work with fear-produced dreams. Fear itself is not always part of the actual dream; it may be active only behind the scenes helping to shape the experience. For example, a woman in her mid-thirties and her husband had recently moved across the country to new jobs, new friends, and a different way of life. It had all been done on intuition, and now things weren't going quite as they had hoped. This is her dream:

> A companion and I are in a snowstorm. We are deep in a wilderness area, having ridden down a cold, rapid river. But I am unwilling to go on down the river any further, because I don't know where it will lead. We decide to get out of the wilderness by car, but before we have driven very far we get stuck in wet snow.

When she awakened she felt quite naturally discouraged. The dream seemed to predict disaster for them in their new environment. But, as she thought about it further, she remembered another approach to interpretation and asked herself: "*Does the dream simply reflect something that I fear?*" In fact, it did. The dream proved not to be predictive of continuing problems, but merely a picture of her fears about things at the time the dream happened. As the months went by she and her husband began to feel more and more at home and things began to work out well for them.

The Cayce readings used this approach in many instances. For example, one woman who very much wanted to get pregnant brought Cayce a dream in which she had been told that she could never conceive a child. The simple story line of this dream might be worded, "Someone is unable to have a child." But how did this simple story line fit her life? Was it a literal message, diagnostic of her actual condition, or was the meaning of the dream more subtle? The reading given for this dream said that it had been produced solely by a mental condition from her waking life—her fears that perhaps she was incapable of getting pregnant. As a fear-produced dream, it had come just to remind her that this fear pattern was present. But she had no need to worry about her physical ability to conceive.

In another case a thirty-two-year-old man asked Cayce to decipher a dream that greatly troubled him: An adversary reminded the dreamer that he had but two years of college and therefore had no right to present himself as someone in possession of knowledge. The Edgar Cayce reading reassured him that it was *not* a literal guidance dream, but rather one produced by his own fears—fears that in his teaching and writing someone might expose his lack of formal education. The real meaning of this dream—and almost all fear-produced or desire-produced dreams—was simply this: work at a conscious level with self-study and prayer to change the mental patterns that show themselves in the dream.

DREAMS WITH A PLAY ON WORDS

You will discover that your dreams often have a sense of humor. Guidance messages may be presented in the form of puns, and finding them can be great fun.

Sometimes the simple story line itself is a play on words. In other cases one small piece of the action is a pun or a single symbol has this kind of double meaning. Let's look first at two examples where the simple story line fit an aspect of the dreamer's life, but the dreamer discovered this match only by seeing the play on words in the dream.

Edgar Cayce once dreamed that he was wading in the water at the beach with his wife, his secretary, and another friend. Cayce ventured out too far and suddenly found himself in water too deep. When he tried to get back, he couldn't. When he called for help, his secretary ran to find someone, and the friend waded out further and tried to help him get back.

A reading was taken to interpret this dream, and from the trancelike state Edgar Cayce offered a meaning for his own dream. The simple story line was, "Someone gets in over his head and has to turn to friends for help." The reading noted how this simple story line was a play on the words "getting in over your head." Cayce was tempted to take on too much, especially in his work. This was to be avoided; but if it happened, he needed to turn to his family and friends for assistance. The dream contained an essential message about the nature of Cayce's life work through the psychic readings: it was through cooperative, concerted efforts that the real work was being done.

In a contemporary example a thirty-six-year-old woman had the following dream:

> I am standing on the very edge of a boulder overlooking a river. All of a sudden the boulder falls off and I tumble down. I am able to maneuver myself cleverly so that the boulder doesn't fall on me and trap me. Friends pull me out of the water, amazed that I haven't been killed.

The simple story line she wrote for this dream used these words: "I go right to the edge and have a dangerous fall." In trying to fit the simple story line to her waking life, she saw a play on words with the phrase "go right to the edge," a slang expression that can mean to test the limits of a situation. She recognized her recent tendency to push situations in her life right to the edge, perhaps dangerously so. The dream seemed to be a warning about doing this. She even saw a second pun in this dream. The phrase "all wet" often means "all wrong." For her the message of the dream was that she was all wrong to dangerously push situations in her life to their limits.

Sometimes the pun in the dream is not found in the simple story line but in a single image. Remember the dream described in chapter one, in which a woman with health problems dreamed that it was raining laundry starch? Cayce interpreted it as a play on words: she needed more starchy foods in her diet.

A twenty-seven-year-old man brought Cayce a dream in which he saw a headless sailor in uniform walk by. The reading interpreted the symbol of headlessness to be a pun: Don't lose your head in performing your duties in life.

One final example shows how you can sometimes discover the message of your dream by seeing puns that come not from the dream images themselves, but from immediate associations which come to mind upon awakening. One business executive in his early forties awakened remembering only that he had dreamed something about the author Pearl Buck. His immediate association was with her novel *The Good Earth*. The words "good earth" struck him as a play on words, a reminder to get back in touch with nature and the soil. The message of this dream fragment appeared to encourage him to balance his life by reconnecting with the earth.

Remember, your goal is to relate your dream to events in your life. Sometimes, with no extra help, you can quickly see how the simple story line fits. However, in other cases, you'll want to ask these five questions:

1. Is this a problem-presentation dream?
2. Is this a compensatory dream that shows me the opposite extreme from what's happening in my life?
3. Is this a dream about my physical health?
4. Is this a dream produced by desires or fears?
5. Is this dream, or a part of it, a play on words?

It is a good idea to try all five approaches, and not settle for just the first one that seems to work. Sometimes a dream will have more than one level of meaning, or multiple messages. Don't stop with the first good interpretation you find. See how many additional, complementary interpretations you can discover.

7

The Meaning of
Dream Symbols

MANY OF THE MOST mysterious dream elements are symbolic: you may encounter people from your childhood about whom you haven't thought for years; you may see strange animals that change from one form to another halfway through the dream; or you may find yourself in places that are an odd mixture of familiar and not so familiar settings. The list of possibilities is endless. It's quite natural for you to wonder, "Is there any way to make heads or tails out of all this confusion?"

A dream dictionary can help; and Part IV of this book is a collection of symbol interpretations given by Edgar Cayce in dream readings. But that is only a starting point. To find the meaning of your own dream symbols will usually take a little more work.

What *is* a dream symbol? The Cayce readings seem to agree with this definition offered by Carl Jung in his extensive dream psychology writings: a dream symbol is the best possible representation of a complex fact not yet grasped by consciousness.

A dream symbol is the very *best* way for your unconscious self to communicate to your conscious self. The particular image chosen—be it an object, a person, an animal, or whatever—has shades of meaning and personal associations that make it the best communicator of some truth about yourself.

But what kind of fact is being communicated? What sort of truth is expressed? It is always something not yet fully understood or grasped by your conscious mind. A dream symbol always comes to expand your knowledge beyond what it was before the dream happened. Edgar Cayce's dream interpretation readings distinguish three types of dream symbol: as sign, as emblem, and as archetype.

DREAM SYMBOLS AS SIGNS

A *sign* points to just one thing; it has just one specific meaning for the dreamer. A sign is often literal, lacking the richness of multiple shades of meaning found in the other two types of dream symbol.

For example, a man in his early twenties asked Edgar Cayce to interpret this dream: "I saw a leak of what seemed to be liquor on our foyer rug, out of a bottle or keg." Cayce interpreted the dream image of liquor to be a sign. It pointed to just a single thing, in this case to liquor itself. The dream was a warning about indiscreet use of alcohol at home. If the dream image had been one of the other two types of dream symbol, then it might have had many other, more subtle meanings (relaxation, sociability, a pun on the word "spirits," and so forth). But in this instance, the dream image was acting merely as a sign.

A man in his mid-forties brought Edgar Cayce this dream to interpret: "My business partner came to me and wanted to use an empty bottle, so I went down into my basement to find one. There I found an old bottle with a large amount of paper money nearby." Cayce's interpretation was that both of the key images in this dream were signs. It was a business dream that showed how he and his partner could have a financial success. The image of a bottle in the dream pointed literally to something they could discover, manufacture, and bottle for sale. The image of money pointed to a single fact in the dreamer's life: considerable money could be made from such a venture.

DREAM SYMBOLS AS EMBLEMS

The second type of dream symbol, the *emblem*, is by far the most frequent type of dream image. Emblems are rich in possible meanings. Those meanings are personal, whereas archetypal symbols are universal and have the same interpretation for everyone. Your emblematic dream symbols require an exploration of your own unique associations and memories, which may be attached to the person, object, place, or animal depicted in the dream.

An emblematic dream symbol usually represents an aspect of yourself. A novice dream interpreter will sometimes find this hard to swallow. It takes a certain amount of courage and humility to admit that some of the images in our dreams refer to elements within ourselves. But the more we work with our dreams, the more we are able to see just how true this is.

In order to capture a fact about ourselves accurately, an emblematic dream symbol will sometimes have a dynamic, changing quality. A dream character will shift into a different person halfway through the dream, or a specific place will inexplicably transform itself into a different setting. This kind of flexibility illustrates how our unconscious, dreaming self is trying to find just the right way to communicate some complex yet very important truth about ourselves.

An example of this is apparent in a dream brought to Edgar Cayce by a college woman:

> I am riding to college on a streetcar. As I ride, I am thinking about some difficult problems in my lessons which I haven't been able to complete. An impudent young man stares at me throughout the ride. When I and two other college women get off the bus, so does he. He follows me, apparently to upset me, and so I ask the two women if I can walk with them for safety. Finally, the young man approaches me, and I am surprised to see that he has changed. No longer is he someone who wants to do me harm; he is now someone who wants to help me with my difficult school lessons.

Edgar Cayce's interpretation was that this transformation of a dream symbol represented a change in attitude, which she was encouraged by the dream to make. The emblematic dream symbol of the young man stood for opportunities and conditions to be met in her life—ones that could be seen either as threatening or as helpful. Here is a contemporary example of an emblem that transformed itself in a dream. It is the dream of a man in his late thirties:

> I am at a museum aquarium. I see a woman sitting on the bottom of the large tank, occasionally floating to the top. She is in labor for childbirth. I go into the tank and offer to be helpful by rubbing her back. Then the setting alters, and I realize we are in the labor and delivery area of a hospital. The woman in labor appears to be my own sister. For a moment, as the dream ends, I become the woman in labor and feel that I am going to deliver the baby.

Not only does this dream illustrate the way in which an emblematic dream symbol can change itself, but it also dramatically shows how a dream character is likely to be a part of oneself. At the end of the dream this man actually experienced how the dream image of his own sister really represented a part of himself. He *became* her for a moment. In this instance he interpreted his dream to concern his own "midlife crisis," which was just beginning. He realized that he was in the early stages of giving birth to a new image of himself—one that had roots in the feminine, feeling side of himself.

Do the people who appear in our dreams *always* represent aspects of ourselves? According to the Cayce readings, the answer is no. Many times we dream psychically about other people, and we'll look closely at that in chapter ten. Probably with the greatest frequency, however, dream characters are emblematic of an aspect of our own personalities. Many of Cayce's dream interpretations illustrate this. For example:

> I am trapped inside a schoolhouse that has been set afire by one of the teachers. When I finally escape the burning building I confront the arsonist. I learn that this disturbed man has started the fire as a kind of revenge against students, who had repeatedly insulted him.

The Cayce reading interpreted the arsonist to be that side of the dreamer which was easily hurt and resentful whenever someone criticized the ideas he tried to teach. The fire symbolized the dreamer's own anger in waking life, which usually was aroused by ridicule. The reading concluded that the message conveyed by this dream was that he should control himself in situations where other people disagreed with his ideas.

That same man had a later dream:

> I am at a meeting of prominent men—scholars, philosophers, and other great minds—who govern the affairs of many people. I stand up to address those men, but suddenly I notice that my own brother is missing. This realization upsets me so much that I break down and cry, and am unable to deliver my speech.

The interpretation offered in the Cayce reading described the image of his brother as an emblem. It represented that side of himself which possessed certain traits just like those of his brother: stability of purpose and intent. This was the key feature in the message of the dream. If the dreamer was to have a positive and influential effect in the world, he needed to get back in touch with this missing characteristic, which was easy to see in his brother.

As you try to interpret the meaning of a dream character, try asking yourself this question: *What traits, positive and negative, do I see in this individual?* This is often the most direct way to find the part of yourself symbolized by that dream character. Of course, this technique will work only when the dream character is someone you know, such as the brother in the dream above. In the previous dream the arsonist resembled no one familiar from the dreamer's waking life. In that case the meaning of the dream symbol could be deciphered only by looking at the way he *acted* in the dream. Another example of such an anonymous dream character is shown in the following dream of a twenty-one-year-old woman:

> I am in a house with my mother and husband. Outside I hear the noise of a rainstorm, as well as shooting and people yelling in excitement. I rush to shut and lock all the windows. As I look out the window, I see a terrible wild man running through the town, shooting a gun and causing great trouble. The police are chasing him.

The simple story line of this dream could be worded, "Someone is causing great turmoil." But where in the dreamer's waking life would this theme fit? Edgar Cayce's interpretation related it to the turmoil she was creating by her uncontrolled anger. The wild man who went around shooting up the town and causing problems for everyone around him symbolized the dreamer herself—her own temper!

Emblematic dream symbols do not always depict our negative traits. Certainly we may often want to ignore our faults, and so these facts about ourselves come to light at night in our dreams. Just as often, however, dream emblems may remind us of our positive qualities. The following story from the files of Cayce readings shows this point. It is the dream of a forty-two-year-old man:

> I am standing on the front porch of a mountain cabin. I hear an explosion and look down the hill just in time to see a man fall to the ground from a gunshot wound. Farther away I see another man holding a smoking rifle. To my amazement the wounded man gets up and starts to run away, but the man with the rifle shoots him again. This happens several times, and the victim always gets back up and runs.

Even though the wounded man was unfamiliar to the dreamer, his actions were a symbolic message about the dreamer's life. The Cayce reading noted the resiliency of the victim—his capacity to keep on going even when he had been hurt. It concluded that this was a dream about business life that showed the reversals and losses that the dreamer had recently incurred. It served to remind him of his own ability to bounce back from adversity. And, even though there would be a point at which such losses would be very detrimental, it promised that more hopeful economic events lay ahead for his business.

DREAM SYMBOLS AS TRUE SYMBOLS OR ARCHETYPES

Dream interpretations would be far easier for us if all symbols had universal meanings and we could rely solely on dream dictionaries. Unfortunately, this is not the case. *Some* of our dream symbols— probably a small minority—are such archetypal images. But the greater number are emblematic, and we must create our own dream dictionary entries to describe their personalized meanings.

Nevertheless, it is fun and instructive to look at dream symbols that may have the same interpretation for everyone. As you look through and study Part IV of this book—the Edgar Cayce Dream Symbol Dictionary—you will see references to many of these universal symbols. For example, look at the entries for these symbols: baby, blood, bread, death, fire, moon, sun, water.

As you read these selections and others, you'll notice that a symbol that *could* be universal *isn't always*. For example, water in your dream might represent the source of all life. If so, it would be acting as an archetypal image in this particular dream. But suppose that in childhood you developed a fear of water because of a near-drowning episode. In another dream, the image of water might not serve as an archetypal symbol at all, but could represent fear.

Sometimes an animal in your dreams has a universal meaning. For example, a man brought to Edgar Cayce a dream in which he saw three elephants. Cannonballs were shooting out of their mouths from under their tusks. For *this* dream Cayce interpreted an elephant in terms of a universal symbol—an archetype that represents knowledge and power. But such a meaning wouldn't always fit, for this particular dreamer or *any* dreamer. In other experiences the dream symbol of an elephant might correspond to certain personal associations with elephants.

It is this characteristic of dreams and their symbols that gives them their special flavor. This elusive, paradoxical trait can be seen in two ways, depending on your point of view. You can get frustrated with your dreams because it is hard to pin down "once and for all" what a particular symbol means. Or you can see this ambiguous, ever-changing characteristic as a reflection of the richness of dream life—how dreams explore the complex features of your life. Your dreams will be more fun to work with if you adopt the second perspective.

But even with the positive outlook, you'll still need some help when it comes to picking the right meaning from among several possibilities for a particular symbol. That help comes most often from the simple story line approach. It allows you to find the *aspect* of your life that the dream probably addresses. Then you can ask yourself, "For this part of my life, which of the possible meanings is most relevant?"

Suppose that you have had two dreams several nights apart, and both dreams contain the symbol of blood. In the dream dictionary you'll find at least seven possible meanings. Before you try to guess which ones fit the two dreams, it would be best to write simple story lines for each dream. Suppose the results look like this: The simple story line of dream 1 is, "Someone is trying to force something to work harder than it can." The simple story line of dream 2 is, "Someone is rediscovering something about another person."

Next, imagine that you look for a place where simple story line 1 fits your waking life, and you find that it corresponds to the way in which you have been treating your physical body. Now you have found the aspect of your life that is probably being addressed by the dream. Which of the seven possible meanings for blood would best fit in this area of your life? You might choose from the dream dictionary: "the physical forces of the body itself, indicative of the relative level of health or imbalance."

On the other hand, you will probably find that the symbol of blood has a different meaning for the second dream. Imagine that you take simple story line 2 and look for a place where it fits your waking life. Suppose that theme corresponds to what is happening in an interpersonal relationship that is slowly being healed after a long-standing resentment. Having found the most likely part of your life addressed by the second dream, you can now try to interpret the symbol of blood in that specific context. You might choose this possibility from the dream dictionary: "kinship (as in 'blood ties')." In this case, the image of blood reminds you of the bonds that you can feel with this other person.

HOW TO CREATE YOUR OWN DREAM DICTIONARY

You can develop skills for finding personal dream symbol interpretations. You'll want to learn and practice these techniques, because no dream dictionary can tell you everything you'll need to know. Sometimes you'll want to add possibilities that aren't listed in the dream dictionary. Other times you'll discover that a particular symbol isn't even listed in the dictionary and you have to start from scratch.

For example, suppose that you had a dream in which a rhinoceros played a key role. After you find the simple story line and try to relate it to your life, you are still going to want to discover the specific meaning of a rhinoceros. What is the message that this particular image is trying to reveal to you?

When you look in the Edgar Cayce Dream Symbol Dictionary, you'll find no entry for rhinoceros. No one ever presented a dream to Cayce for interpretation that had this symbol in it. Because of just this sort of limitation, you'll want to use the three techniques described below for finding personal interpretations: amplification, interviewing, and role playing.

Amplification

The first technique is *amplification*, proposed by Carl Jung (see his *Collected Works, Volume 4*, pages 144–148 for a description of the rationale). It's a form of free association in which you let descriptive words and feelings pop into your mind. Let's look at an example.

A thirty-two-year-old man had the following dream:

> A giant comes through the door and I throw an iron poker at him. I attack the giant repeatedly with the poker, but it has no effect. The giant threatens to hit me with his huge fist.

Before we see how the Cayce reading interpreted the symbol of a giant for this dreamer, let's imagine how we might go about finding its meaning without the help of a psychic or dream dictionary. If it were your own dream, what would it mean to *you*?

A good place to start is always the simple story line. Perhaps you might word it, "Something big is threatening me." If you cannot see how this relates to your waking life, you go on to explore clues from personal associations with the image of a giant.

The amplification technique invites you to let thoughts and feelings freely come into your mind. This kind of free association, however, always comes back to the dream symbol rather than drifting off into an irrelevant sidetrack. You might jot down on a piece of paper associations like these:

* A giant is big.
* A giant is often mean.
* A giant is usually misunderstood.
* A giant is strong.
* A giant has difficulty making friends.
* A giant makes everyone else feel small.
* A giant always seems to lose at the end of fairy tales.

To create a list of associations to amplify one of your own dream symbols, try asking yourself the following five questions about the symbol. These questions were proposed by Gayle Delaney in *Living Your Dreams* and by G. Scott Sparrow in *Awakening the Dreamer*. Fill in the blank space with the symbolic object, place, animal, or person's name.

1. What is a _____?
2. What does a _____ do?
3. What does a _____ remind you of?
4. What do you like about a _____?
5. What do you dislike about a _____?

Certainly, not all the associations you come up with will be useful or relevant for interpreting the dream. However, when you amplify a symbol, a *few* of the associations that come to mind will have a certain feeling of rightness. They may be accompanied by a sense of discovery; you may get an intuitive feeling that you are on to something. Most often, after getting a dozen or more free associations this way, only one or two of them will seem to be especially significant.

In the giant dream, we have the benefit of Edgar Cayce's psychic perceptions. The reading indicated that a giant was something that makes everything else feel small. More precisely, the dreamer had recently been ridiculed for espousing his unorthodox beliefs, and the giant symbolized the pressures and influence of that condemnation.

Interviewing

A second technique to find personal associations for dream symbols is the *interview*, described in detail by Gayle Delaney in her book *Living Your Dreams*. It is a specific development of the amplification approach. One thing that makes Delaney's method so helpful is the set of questions posed by a hypothetical visitor to earth. In describing the rationale for dream symbol amplification, Jung was never very specific about technique. Delaney's approach makes it all highly practical.

Imagine that you have to describe the dream symbol in question to an alien who has just arrived from another planet and knows nothing about the earth. The alien will interview you concerning the object, place, animal, or person that was used as a symbol in your dream. This space traveler is likely to ask some or all of the following seven questions. As before, the blank space is for the name of the symbol.

1. What is _____?
2. What kind of person would use _____ or be involved with it in some way?
3. How is _____ produced?
4. What benefits does _____ provide?
5. What problems does _____ create for others?
6. What are the advantages of having _____?
7. What are the disadvantages of having _____?

Your alien may be quite creative and think of many other probing questions besides these seven. The point of the technique is to strip away familiar assumptions and get right to the core of what a particular symbol is all about from your own point of view.

Role Playing

A third technique to find personal associations for dream symbols is *role playing*, an approach pioneered by Fritz Perls as part of his psychotherapeutic method called Gestalt therapy. It involves *becoming the symbol* momentarily and experiencing the world through the imaginary eyes of that symbolic object, person, or other living thing. This method makes great sense when we remember that often our dream symbols do in fact represent us.

The following three questions are particularly useful for this technique. You can ask yourself these questions, or have a friend ask them. Each question should be asked several times, because your first response often will not reveal the deeper levels of meaning and association you want to tap.

1. As _____, how do you feel about what is going on in the dream?
2. As _____, how do you feel about yourself?
3. As _____, what do you want or desire?

Your answers must tap into the feeling level. Intellectual, analytical statements will not be very productive. Spontaneous feelings are more likely to offer insight into the meaning of the specific symbol you are role playing.

In order to successfully understand your dream symbols, you'll need to keep a playful, exploratory attitude. Almost every dream symbol—especially the two types we have called emblems and universal symbols—are rich in subtle meanings. No single word or phrase accurately captures *all* of what it conveys and reveals to you. Not only does the symbol contain within it a message your intellectual mind can grasp; it also works on you at a nonverbal, emotional level.

You will also need to keep a delicate balance between two attitudes. On the one hand, it is often very rewarding to "figure out" what a dream symbol meant. Dream dictionaries may assist you in getting started; using the three techniques described near the end of this chapter will take you even farther. But you must also remember where dreams come from: your own unconscious, soul-self. Dreams and their symbols originate at a level within you that is much more vast and dynamic than your conscious mind can imagine. And so you must also *appreciate* the dream symbol, *listen* to it, and *honor* its reality and importance. You can do this by *feeling deeply* the quiet, transforming effect it had upon you in the dream. With that kind of balanced attitude and approach you will make friends with your dream symbols and allow them to teach you.

PART III

Psychic and Spiritual Dreams

8

The Reality of
Your Dream Experiences

How vivid and real some dreams seem to be! Have you ever awakened in the morning unsure which world was more real to you—the familiar physical environment or the realm of dreams you just left? Have you ever had a dream in which the people and the place felt so authentic that it was hard to call the experience "just a dream"?

Nearly everyone has had a taste of just how real dreams can be, but exactly what does this mean? Surely we shouldn't act out in waking life every one of our dreams. How *should* we understand dream reality? The answer lies in exploring three different kinds of experience that emphasize the reality of dreams: (1) *lesson dreams*, which put us into instructive situations; (2) *peak spiritual dreams*, which may give us a taste of higher dimensions of reality; and (3) *contact with deceased individuals* through dreams. For each, little or no interpretation is needed. *The experience itself is the meaning of the dream.*

LESSON DREAMS: HOW ARE YOU DOING IN NIGHT SCHOOL?

We have already seen how our dreams teach us to be more effective in daily life. Most often we must do some knowledgeable interpretation after awakening from the dream in order to learn those lessons. But sometimes the lessons are presented in a way that requires no interpretation. Think about how an especially gifted teacher might instruct his or her students. Merely teaching facts is not likely to be the most efficient method. Instead, this teacher skillfully provides *real experiences* for the students—situations and events that will produce changes in them.

Some of your dreams will become clear if you think through the answer to this question: *"If* this had been a waking life experience, how would I have been changed by it?" The change you are looking for may be a new attitude or emotion, a different perspective on a problem, or a new feeling about yourself or someone else.

This sort of lesson dream is a real experience because the changes it makes in you are *real.* It carries over into your waking life and may profoundly alter the way you respond to life. In fact, this method of looking at a dream is so important that the Edgar Cayce dream interpretation readings often used it. As examples, look at this series of three dreams of a man in his early thirties, a wealthy stockbroker from New York City. (The first dream was discussed in chapter five, pages 59–60.)

> I am in a hurry, driving my car very fast along a highway. I notice that someone I have passed has written down my license number. Soon thereafter I am stopped by a policeman for speeding. Just before awakening, I ask myself, "What is the use of hurrying if you are held up on the road this way?"

The simple story line—"Trying to rush things results in a big delay"—is one good way to get at the meaning of this dream. The dreamer might have been able to find a part of his daily life in which rushing was counterproductive, but he might just as easily have approached the interpretation of this dream by seeing it as a *real* experience. But real in what way? Are there truly automobiles and policemen in the higher dimensions of mind from which dreams come? Will the dreamer really have to pay that speeding ticket in a later dream, or else really face going to a dream jail?

Of course, that line of questioning is absurd. Yet, in another way, the dream and its impact were real. It directly changed the man's attitudes and approach to life. Suppose he had asked himself this question: "*If* this had been a waking life experience, how would I have been changed by it?" Surely his answer would have been a strong feeling about the wisdom of taking his time and not being in a hurry. This was exactly the advice given by the Cayce reading, and this was the very real lesson he had already learned in the dream—simply by having gone through the events. His second dream is especially entertaining:

> I hear a knock at my front door, and my maid announces that God has come for a visit. I rush to the door and, sure enough, there is God. We embrace, and then I notice that God is a tall, well-built man, clean cut and clean shaven, wearing a brown suit and carrying a gray derby hat. He has an intelligent look and a firm expression. He looks like a healthy, robust businessman. I show him around the house and introduce him to my mother and brother.

Cayce interpreted this dream to be a lesson in which the man had had a very real experience: he had actually made contact with God. This is not to say that God looks like a businessman, but that an authentic view of the qualities of God came through this dream. There is an aspect of God that is fully present here with us in the earth. God is active and alive in the midst of material, even commercial, affairs. God is not to be understood in a sentimental way, but as someone you can "do business with."

Suppose the man had not been able to take his dream to Edgar Cayce for an interpretation? Might he had arrived at this same understanding by himself, just as we usually rely on ourselves to decipher dreams? Perhaps he would have, if he had asked himself, "How was I changed by this experience?" The answer is simple and direct. The dream had stimulated new feelings and new understandings about the nature of God. It wasn't necessary to figure out what the maid symbolizes, or what a gray derby hat means. The dream itself was a real experience, and to recognize its impact is all that is needed upon awakening.

The third and final dream of this series was rather frightening:

I am with my brother and my uncle, who is in poor health and doesn't believe in psychic matters. A mail carrier delivers a package for us that contains a deadly, poisonous scorpion. We are warned not to touch it. Instead, we attach a piping contraption to it and drain a fluid from it, which proves to be a healing agent for my uncle.

Again, this dream had a certain reality. If this same experience had happened in waking life, the lesson would be clear: that which is dangerous can also be a source of healing and life. This is exactly the insight provided in Cayce's interpretation. The dream had come to have an immediate and direct impact on the thoughts and understandings of the dreamer. It was unnecessary to use a symbol dictionary to look up meanings for scorpion, piping, or poison. The importance and message of this dream was to be found in the changed outlook it produced, which then carried over into waking life.

Let's examine another dream, brought to Cayce by a twenty-seven-year-old man:

I am at the seashore with my family. I go out to the ocean's edge and try to dive into a breaker. But instead of landing in the water, I go headfirst into the sand and get stuck. My wife sees my predicament and calls for help. They pull on my feet to get me out, but I feel myself suffocating in the sand.

No symbol interpretation is required; the simple story line approach might be useful, but in this instance there is a more direct way to get at the dream's meaning. If this had happened to him in waking life, what lesson would he have learned? Not to dive into things. It's as simple as that. The same lesson was the one learned from going through these events in the dream world. The very real change of attitude and understanding produced by this experience was meant to carry over into waking life. Or, as his reading from Cayce concluded, " . . . *wade* in, rather than dive in head first. For little by little, line upon line, must one gain . . . " (no. 137–84).

A contemporary example illustrates this same way of working with a dream. This dreamer was an office manager in her late forties:

I am at my high school graduation, where one of my best friends from waking life is acting as the emcee. The next event on the agenda is the presentation of the leadership award. The emcee announces to all in attendance that it will be no surprise who is going to receive this award. It will go to the person who most deserves it. Then I am named to come on stage and be honored with this recognition.

One good way to approach this dream is to see it as a real experience. Something happened in this dream that literally changed the thoughts, feelings, and actions of the woman in her waking life. She realized that she was truly doing a good job with her life. It was not necessary to translate symbols to see this level of meaning in the dream. The message was the experience itself.

PEAK SPIRITUAL EXPERIENCES IN DREAMS

On rare occasions a dream may give you a glimpse of higher dimensions of reality. These peak spiritual experiences require no interpretation: the experience itself is the meaning of the dream.

These kinds of dreams are easy to recognize because of their profound effect. You are likely to awaken inspired, reenergized, and totally uplifted. The Edgar Cayce readings usually called them "visions," although you may need to alter slightly the associations you have had with this word. Most people think of visions as the exclusive domain of saints, and the word connotes mystical perceptions of the spiritual world or ghostly apparitions of higher beings. But, for the Cayce readings, a "vision" is within everyone's reach; it describes those special dream experiences in which we contact directly the higher levels within us.

Edgar Cayce himself sometimes had this kind of experience. Here is one peak spiritual dream that occurred just two years before his death. A reading to interpret this dream was never done, probably because none was necessary:

He dreamed that he was playing solitaire at his home in the evening, when there was a knock at the door and a stranger appeared. The man insisted that Cayce come with him, and they went outside to walk toward the ocean. Another man joined them and when they got to the ocean, they just kept on walking—up, up into the sky. They arrived at a place with a large circus tent and went in. As they entered the tent, Cayce suddenly realized that his two companions were famous evangelists of his youth (but now deceased): Dwight L. Moody and Sam Jones.

The tent was full of unfamiliar figures and an unusual light pervaded the place. In the distance he heard lightning and the loud sound of wind, yet nothing stirred. Cayce was told that God was about to speak to them. A voice, clear and strong, said: "*Who will warn my children?*" After a pause, the voice asked the same question again. Out of the throng gathered in the circus tent, Jesus appeared and said: "I will warn my brethren." The answer came back: "No, the time is not yet fulfilled for you to return. But who shall warn my children?"

Then Mr. Moody spoke up and said, "Why not send Cayce, he is there now." And Jesus echoed this idea: "Father, Cayce will warn my brethren." And finally came a grand chorus from all who had gathered: "And we will all help!"

We can only imagine what an impact this dream probably had on Cayce in the waking state. No doubt this was as real for him as anything that happened to him in waking life. It was a direct experience in the dream state of his own spiritual calling.

The dream image of *light* is frequently found in such peak spiritual dreams. We see that symbol in Cayce's dream, and it is found in other dreams for which interpretative readings were given. One young woman dreamed,

> I see a man in a gray beard who is dressed in pure white like a sheep. I am so impressed that I say, "I can't believe it." Then the man pulls my mother by the arm out into the light.

Cayce's interpretation was that she had had a contact with the Christ, the Lamb, the Redeemer. The experience was to show her directly how the Christ can move individuals into that Light, which is mercy and grace.

This woman's husband had a dream in which light played a key role and was indicative of a peak spiritual experience:

> I see a round, colored light in the sky. I know it is another
> consciousness. It speaks to me, identifying itself as the Christ. Then this
> light changes forms and I now see Jesus pass by in his white flowing
> robes. He seems to understand exactly what I need and teaches me a
> brief lesson. Then I rise up and seem to merge my own consciousness
> with that of the Christ.

Cayce confirmed that this had been a real experience. It needed
no interpretation. The events of this encounter and the words spoken
were themselves the meaning.

A contemporary dreamer had a similar experience, in this case
not with Jesus but with Mary, the mother of Jesus. It came at a time
in her life when she faced a particularly difficult career decision, a
perplexing choice between two completely opposite positions:

> I am with the Virgin Mary, whom I know to be my close friend. Mary
> asks about what's going on in my life. When I tell her of my pending
> career decision, Mary insists that we go to see a psychic named Ruth. I
> am reluctant to see a psychic, but Mary assures me that this one is so
> good that years earlier she had predicted the immaculate conception,
> Mary's marriage to Joseph, and the resurrection of Jesus. That makes
> me feel more comfortable. When we meet Ruth, I am very impressed—
> Ruth is everything an enlightened being should be. I pose my career-
> choice question to the psychic, only to get this response, which ends the
> dream: "What a wonderful opportunity you have, and I know you'll
> make the right decision."

It was easy for the dreamer to find the meaning of this experience.
The point was not whether this constituted an authentic contact with
the soul that once lived as Mary. Perhaps that was the case, but it
would be hard to say for sure. But one thing *was* clear: she woke up
from the dream feeling new confidence in her *own* capacity to make
a good decision. In this way the dream had been a real event for her.

A final example shows one more important point about peak
spiritual dreams. It is *not* a prerequisite that they contain light, Jesus,
or the Virgin Mary. Sometimes they contain more ordinary imagery,
yet still come from a deep spiritual level within. An illustration of this
principle comes from the dreams of a friend of Edgar Cayce:

I am walking by a house with Edgar Cayce's secretary, Gladys, who says to me, "They do not pay their rent." Mr. Cayce himself owns the place, and it is quite large and rambling—a typical beach house. As I wander around the place, I come upon a beautiful lake. Its water is clear, and lovely swans are swimming around. Loving, happy children are feeding them. I begin to feel extraordinarily happy and uplifted.

Edgar Cayce's interpretation of this dream reinforces its importance. It does not seem to be a very grandiose experience; there is no overtly religious symbology. And yet Cayce's reading said that this had been a direct contact with her own, highest spiritual ideals. The feelings that had been awakened in her by the dream were genuine, and they indicated the truth and power of the experience for her.

DREAMS AND THE SURVIVAL OF PHYSICAL DEATH

In many ways the conditions we encounter in our dreams resemble the after-death state. There are significant differences, of course, but some dreams can be seen as almost a rehearsal for the consciousness of an afterlife. On more than one occasion, the Cayce readings pointed out for a dreamer how he or she had been given a view of the so-called "borderland" or realm of consciousness in which a soul lives immediately after leaving the physical plane.

None of this is meant to scare us. Such dreams do not necessarily predict impending death. Instead they should reassure us that as souls we feel equally at home in this dimension of life *or* in other dimensions. We will explore this notion with greater depth in the next chapter, when we discuss astral experiences through dreams. But related to this issue are those dreams interpreted by Cayce in which dreamers seem to have contacted deceased friends and loved ones. So: What does it mean when we dream of someone who is dead?

One possibility is to interpret such a dream character just the way we would for one who was still alive. What personality characteristics did you see in this person? What key traits can you remember?

What did you like or dislike about this individual? Such a series of questions may help you see what aspect of *yourself* is symbolized.

Another line of analysis is to ask yourself about unresolved feelings concerning this person's death. The dream image of the deceased person may not represent that soul itself, but rather your own unfinished business connected with that individual's passing. Such a dream then comes as a reminder about inner work you should do on your own attitudes and emotions. Perhaps it will involve forgiveness or greater appreciation.

However, a third possibility also finds frequent support in the Cayce readings. Through our dreams we can actually contact those who have passed on to the borderland. One reading put it most clearly to a forty-eight-year-old widow who asked about frequent dreams of her deceased husband. First came the confirmation that these dreams were often soul-to-soul contacts, then four qualities of such dreams were listed: assistance, guidance, help, and comfort.

Among the listed qualities, "comfort" probably stands out for most people who have lost a close friend or loved one. It is natural to want confirmation that life has continuity. It is interesting to note the kind of dream for which Cayce readings most frequently assured the dreamer of an authentic contact: an experience from which the dreamer awakened with the feeling that love survives the grave; the kind of dream which seemed so real that the dreamer was personally convinced that a genuine contact had been made.

For example, one man who received many Cayce dream readings had recurrent dream experiences with his dead father. In nearly every case the reading suggested that the father appeared in the dream as a guide *and* as a reminder about the continuity of spiritual life. Here is one such dream:

> I see many different beautiful lights, each of which I know intuitively to be a spirit entity. I sense that one is my father. Suddenly, my father takes on a more human form, but with a body of light shining like the sun. He stands at the foot of my bed, and I burst into tears of joy at the closeness of my father. I tell my father that I love him, and I hear my father affirm his own love in return.

Clearly, this special dream needed no ordinary analysis. It was a profound experience that gave the man an unshakable knowledge of life beyond physical death.

Quite naturally, we may look for a second meaning in these special dreams: that a person who has passed on may still be mindful of those left behind. In the philosophy of the Edgar Cayce readings not only are souls in the borderland often mindful of loved ones in the earth plane, they even try to help. A deceased person may recurrently appear in dreams as a source of advice and assistance.

It is reassuring to know that such care and help is offered, but as interpreters we should remember that physical death does not bestow instant enlightenment. *The dream advice that comes from a deceased loved one may well be taken as a real experience, but the apparent guidance will still need to be evaluated.*

For example, ask yourself this: "Is there any living person whom I so trust that I would follow that person's advice, no matter what he or she said?" The answer is probably "no." Advice, even from those whom you most admire for wisdom, still needs to be weighed and judged for helpfulness each time. The same holds true for those who have passed on to another dimension from which they continue to offer help. Make sure the assistance makes good sense, and that it leads you in the direction of your own ideals.

Finally, we should note a word of caution from the Edgar Cayce readings about our ability to contact the dead through dreams. It is best to let such experiences come spontaneously. Do not try to initiate them or force them. The loved one or friend in the borderland is better able than you to see when such contact is useful and needed. In many cases such contact may actually be a hindering distraction for the soul on the other side, who may have a more important agenda to deal with. Or the soul may experience a period of confusion or disorientation immediately after death, which would only be made worse by our attempts. As much as we, the physical survivors, may crave such a contact, our continuing love requires patience. The best that we can do is to be open to receive such an experience—and diligent in trying to remember our dreams so that we can claim it should it come.

9

Dreams of Power: Lucidity, Astral Travel, and Out-of-Body

LUCID DREAMING

Have you ever known you were dreaming *while* the dream was still going on? If so, you know what a remarkable experience it can be. Researchers have named this extraordinary kind of episode *lucid dreaming*. It's an accurate description because most of these dreams are characterized by their clarity. Everything about the dream seems so vivid and real! Sometimes the dreamer discovers that he or she has power to fly or to alter the events in the dream.

Lucid dreaming is one of the most exciting aspects of modern dream research. What sort of person is most likely to have such an experience? Can people learn how to do it? The subject, however, is also controversial. Does lucid awareness upset the natural mental process that goes on in a dream? Is it really wise to manipulate dream events?

Most people remember having had a lucid dream at least once, but they occur rarely for most dreamers. Despite their infrequency, lucid dreams can have a powerful impact. Margaret's dream is a good example:

> I am shopping at my neighborhood grocery store. As I push my cart down the aisles, I notice that the meat department not only has

packaged meats, but live animals as well. The produce department has indoor gardens from which I can pick fresh vegetables, and there are huge fruit trees growing right inside the store!

Suddenly, I remember that I shouldn't be shopping that morning—I should be at school. Today we are having final exams, and I have forgotten all about them. I rush from the store, jump into my car, and head off toward campus. Speeding along, I'm in a panic. Will I be too late? Maybe it doesn't matter whether I'm on time, because I have also forgotten to study for the tests.

Then I recognize that I must have made a wrong turn in my haste. The road looks unfamiliar, and giant palm trees line the street. That is impossible, because I live in Minnesota. Then, suddenly, I realize that I must be dreaming. All of this is just a dream world.

As soon as I discover that I am dreaming, other thoughts come to mind. I remember that I am no longer a college student who years ago had done poorly on some final exams. I am now an adult woman in my mid-fifties. I can relax. There is no need to fear being late to some tests.

I decide to explore this dream world. I'm anxious that I might wake up in bed, but for several more minutes I continue to ride in my dream car. Everything seems so real. The colors and the three-dimensional appearance of things are just like my waking world.

Finally, I decided to abandon my car and walk. I see an open field and begin to run through it. My feet barely seem to touch the ground as I pick up speed. And then, unexpectedly, I begin to fly. At first I am just a few inches off the ground, but suddenly I begin to soar. What an exhilarating feeling!

Although Margaret wished her dream flight could have lasted much longer, she soon awakened at home in bed. But the feelings of power and freedom that had been created in that special dream stayed with her. Throughout that day and for many days thereafter she had a new sense of herself. She made no effort to fly in her normal, physical body, and yet something was unmistakably different about the way she moved through her life.

All lucid dreams have one characteristic in common. At some point, *while the dream is still going on,* you know that you are in a dream world. If you have ever had a lucid dream, you probably know just how special these inner events can be. They are usually so vivid and dramatically different from a normal dream that they are hard to forget. Your experience may have had some of the elements of her lucid dream: starting out as a normal dream, recognizing some impossible feature which then triggers the lucidity, flying in your dream body, and carrying tremendous positive feelings back with you into waking life.

Many other experiences, of course, may occur in a lucid dream. The sudden knowledge that you are dreaming may be initiated by strong fears rather than the recognition of some incongruity. Lucid dreams frequently occur when the dreamer is being pursued by a ferocious animal or a menacing person. The lucidity serves to dispel the fear and bring the reassurance that "all of this is just a dream."

Another feature of lucid dreaming is the dreamer's ability to manipulate or alter the dream symbols and action. Margaret didn't do this, but many lucid dreamers have discovered just how malleable the dream world is to conscious intentions. The lucid dreamer can willfully change one image into another, shaping the dream to be exactly what he or she wants it to be.

Is such dream manipulation wise? Just because it is *possible* to do something doesn't mean that it is best to try it. There is a deep wisdom active in shaping the content of our dreams. Images and symbols appear for a reason, and we should respect that fact. It is really a kind of avoidance process to use the "magic powers" of a lucid dream to manipulate things. Situations arise in our dreams because they represent challenges in need of healing or greater understanding. So-called "dream control" through lucidity can be a trap. By avoiding or removing something unpleasant from a dream, we haven't really dealt with the energies it stands for.

The example of Thomas illustrates a better approach. Thomas is an experienced lucid dreamer who has learned the difference between dream control and self-control. On repeated occasions he has found that changing his own *reaction* to what is happening in the dream has an indirect effect on the appearance of the dream images themselves.

For example, one night he had a frightening dream in which he was chased by a pack of wild dogs. He couldn't see the dogs but he could hear their vicious barking, which seemed to follow him no matter where he ran. Then, in the depths of his panic, he realized that it was all a dream. Just as this lucidity emerged the dogs came into view for the first time. They saw him too and began a mad dash across the open spaces toward him. Rather than use his powers of dream lucidity to change the ferocious dogs into something more pleasant, he chose to stand his ground and *change his fear*.

He reminded himself that he was in a dream body that could not be hurt, and he tried to hold a compassionate, loving attitude toward the wild animals. This inner change had an immediate impact on the outward form of the dream. The wild dogs came right up to him and began to lick him playfully. Their affection reminded him of his favorite dog from childhood, and he woke feeling he had befriended the renegade, rejected side of himself.

This kind of positive, healing potential from our dreams is what we have come to expect as we have examined how Edgar Cayce's readings interpreted dreams. The term "lucid dreaming" is relatively new. It was not used in Cayce's time, and there are very few instances in which dreamers brought to Cayce this kind of experience, no matter what they might have called it. In fact, only two clear examples of lucid dreams are interpreted in Cayce readings.

The first case concerns a forty-four-year-old man who was in the real estate business. His experience clearly shows how lucidity can help to solve a problem in the dream state:

I am in a train station in Kansas City during a stopover on the way to Chicago. I am exercising my legs from the long ride by walking up and down along the platform beside my train, when I remember that I have left my overcoat in the depot. I worry that if I go back inside the train might leave without me. Suddenly, the train starts to move. I try to run alongside to get back into my car, but I can't make headway. Then I realize that I must be dreaming, since it would be impossible in waking life to be stuck that way when trying to run. With this realization I am released and I easily catch up with my train.

Unfortunately, if we hope to learn more from Cayce about lucid dreaming from this example, we are disappointed, because he provided no insights. The interpretation in the reading did not even refer to the remarkable change that happened at the end of the dream. Instead, the man was told that his dream concerned certain business affairs and literally related to his dealings with commercial interests in railroads.

The second example comes from one of Edgar Cayce's own lucid dreams, which he had interpreted in a reading. This particular experience came when he was fifty years old. He dreamed that his dead grandmother was alive again and he planned to give her a reading. He found her with vines growing all around and over her. His wife, Gertrude, and his secretary, Gladys, helped him to cut away the vines. But as they finished the work and began to leave, they were confronted by three stray dogs. One dog got away and began to run back toward the grandmother's body, and Cayce the dreamer gave chase. All of a sudden he knew that he was dreaming *and he knew what the dream meant*: in waking life they were letting their work "go to the dogs" as they got involved in things they had no business doing.

The reading given for this dream reinforced the insight that came at its end. Regrettably, nothing else was given regarding the unusual state we know as lucid dreaming. However, this dream does offer to us a valuable illustration of one key principle: lucidity may be an effective tool for determining what a dream means *while it is still going on*.

ASTRAL PROJECTION AND OUT-OF-BODY TRAVEL

Even though the Cayce readings have little to say about lucid dreaming, there is considerable material about its close "cousin," astral projection—people who received Cayce readings were far more fascinated with this remarkable experience. Happily, many of the discoveries we can make about astral projection are equally true for lucid dreaming. In fact, it is often hard to distinguish between the two.

What is *astral projection* or, as it is sometimes called, *out-of-body experience?* Cayce's readings and many other sources claim that we have more than one body. Obviously, we have physical bodies; but not so obvious are subtle bodies composed of higher forms of energy. We find references in esoteric literature to the etheric body and to the astral body and it is likely that other bodies of even higher vibration probably exist as well.

What evidence is there for an etheric and astral body? Mainstream science sees none; but there are data from the laboratory that suggest that we don't yet fully understand all the energy configurations that are associated with the human body.

For example, Kirlian photography, a form of electrophotography, has repeatedly demonstrated the existence of invisible energy patterns that surround the physical body. In demonstrations of Kirlian photography, a high-voltage electrical field interacts with objects to produce the image of an encompassing energy field on the film. The interpretation of these results is an open debate. But even if Kirlian photography does not take an exact picture of etheric energy, it does show the limitations of traditional assumptions about the body.

Another kid of evidence comes from clairvoyants, Edgar Cayce and dozens of others. Psychically sensitive people provide remarkably similar reports about what they can see in and around the human body. For example, the aura has been described by psychics for hundreds of years. It extends beyond the physical body and can be understood as an aspect of the etheric and astral bodies.

In waking life, these subtle bodies interpenetrate the physical body. But at night, as we sleep and dream, the astral body separates from the physical body and can explore independently both the physical world and the astral realms. This happens to everyone, every night. Cayce once put it bluntly: "Each and every soul leaves the body as it rests in sleep" (no. 853–8).

But even though such astral trips are commonplace, rarely are they *conscious* experiences that we remember afterward. Apparently our soul experiences are created in such a way that we recall only a small portion of what happens to us each night.

What, then, is the meaning or significance of the extraordinary events called astral projection or out-of-body travel? Here are the two types of experience that most frequently receive such labels: (1) the astral body moves out of the physical body and independently experiences the *physical world*; (2) the astral body moves into a nonphysical world and the astral traveler *lucidly* experiences this higher dimension.

An example of the first type of event is the near-death experience. *Life After Life* by Raymond Moody and *Heading Toward Omega* by Kenneth Ring report on surveys of hundreds of the many people who have had this experience. One often-repeated feature is projecting out of the dying physical body and looking back at it from a distance. People who experience this usually report that they subsequently lose all fear of physical death, having felt so directly the reality of another body.

But even more frequently this can happen from the sleep state. An illustration of this process can be found in one Cayce reading where a man asked about astral projection. While asleep he projected his astral body to North Carolina, where he conversed with an old friend. She reported sometime later that she had actually felt a contact with his presence at the same time. In his reading the man asked Edgar Cayce if he should try to have this happen more often.

The reading cautioned against it. It said such experiences were fine, but should be viewed as a *natural result* of the way he was living his life, rather than some curiosity to be attempted.

The second type of experience resembles a lucid dream. In fact, this kind of astral projection is probably indistinguishable from a lucid dream. Here the events do not take place in the familiar physical dimension but occur in another level of spiritual existence. What makes it remarkable is *conscious self-reflection*: knowing that you are in the midst of an extraordinary experience while it is still going on.

Later, you might well look back on the experience and ask yourself, "*Where* did it all happen?" The answer cannot be given in spatial terms. Instead, it might be said that it all took place within you, the dreamer—within you, the astral projectionist. Or the answer might be that it took place beyond time and space as we normally know them.

For example, one woman brought to Edgar Cayce the following remarkable out-of-body experience: During a surgical operation, while she was thought to have died, she traveled astrally first to California, and then to "realms of light." She asked in her reading, "Where did I go really and what was the meaning and purpose of the experience?" (no. 2067–3).

The reading stated that the entire projection had been *within herself*. It had not been a delusion; but no spatial distance had been covered. She had traveled in a higher energy body. In that nonphysical body she had been able to see and later remember dimensions of consciousness usually invisible. And what did it mean for her? The reading stated that all this had been presented to show her the oneness of consciousness that comes in the Light. The purpose of this out-of-body trip was to show her directly a greater truth about herself and all of life.

The following story of a contemporary astral projectionist demonstrates both types of experience: moving spatially with the astral body through the physical world, *and* projecting into a nonphysical dimension.

Elizabeth was a twenty-five-year-old graduate student involved in intense studies of modern philosophy. Each day she spent hours and hours reading and debating the minute points of contemporary philosophers. Most of the material focused on reducing human existence to logical and material concerns. The side of Elizabeth that was interested in spiritual matters was put on the "back burner" for awhile. But apparently as a counterbalancing effect, she began to have remarkable astral-projection experiences. These inner events seem to come as a sort of compensation for the one-sided extremes of her philosophy studies.

First came an experience that started as a normal dream:

> I am standing in a glass house, leaning on one of the glass walls. It begins to fall and is transformed into a magic carpet that takes me for a ride into the sky. Initially, this flight is fun, and I suddenly realize that I

am in a dream world. But the carpet ride quickly becomes frightening when it soars out of the earth's atmosphere and into outer space. Even though I know that I am having an astral projection, it is out of my control and I'm afraid. To my relief the magic carpet turns back toward home, just as it is approaching the sun. Moments later it brings me back to earth and to my physical body. As I move back into my body, I have a feeling of falling. Then I awaken in my bed.

This experience fits the second of the two categories. It is indistinguishable from a lucid dream and (despite the reference to the earth and the sun) probably took place in nonphysical dimensions. The fact that it began in a glass house that resembles none known to her in waking life suggests as much.

She had two other astral projections soon thereafter, and both fit the first category. In one she saw herself sit up in bed while her physical body was still asleep. She got up in her astral body and went into her study, where she sat at her desk and worked on a philosophy paper that had to be written the next day. Upon awakening the next morning she remembered this out-of-body trip, and even found that when she sat down at her desk to write, she knew just the words to use.

The other astral trip resembled the previous one, but in this instance she went up on her roof and sat for part of the night, watching activities at the sorority across the street. What she remembered seeing that night matched the physical events taking place—things that were happening as her familiar body slept in bed.

Seven Guidelines

The Cayce readings offered seven guidelines about what to keep in mind and what to do to ensure safe and helpful out-of-body experiences:

1. *Let the experiences come as a natural outgrowth of spiritual attunement.* Remember this advice given to the man who astrally traveled to North Carolina in his sleep? It means to let go of fear concerning astral projections or out-of-body trips, but it also means

to avoid forcing them to happen before you are ready. Simply be open for the possibility.

2. *Get your physical body into the best state of health that you can.* Strange as it may sound, a healthy *physical* body may make things easier and safer for projections of your nonphysical body. Cayce said to one woman who was interested in out-of-body travel: "First, do those things that will make [your] body . . . WHOLE. Projections, inflections, astral experiences, are much harder upon those who are not *wholly* physically fit" (no. 516–4).

3. *The secret of how to have out-of-body experiences during sleep is simple.* The basic, empowering force is love. The guiding force is the spirit of truth. What does Cayce mean by that? Astral projection can be anticipated as a natural result whenever you sincerely hold love as an ideal in your life—not just for your dream life but for everything you do. Furthermore, you can be assured of a positive experience if your commitment is to a search for truth instead of fanciful diversions. Astral travel is not meant to be something you merely add to your list of accomplishments and entertainment, like vacations you've taken or movies you've seen. This extraordinary kind of experience has the potential to show you directly the deeper truths of who you are.

4. *Regular meditation increases the likelihood of astral-projection experiences.* The *purpose* of meditation should be attunement for spiritual growth reasons. But an outcome of enhanced attunement of body, mind, and spirit may well be lucid dreams, out-of-body experiences, or astral projections. For many people the most effective time of day to meditate in order to foster these inner events is during the night.

You can experiment with the time that works best for you (for example, sometime between 2:00 A.M. and 4:00 A.M.). It is important to have gotten several hours of sleep first. The first few days it will probably be difficult to stay awake and meditate, but as you get used to being up at that time, it will become easier to stay alert. Follow your normal approach to meditation—don't meditate upon your desire for astral projection. Then, after completing your meditation session, go back to sleep. When you are properly attuned and ready at all levels for an experience, it will come.

5. *As you are falling asleep, if you feel that you may have a conscious astral projection, surround yourself with light.* Provide yourself with a protective influence anytime you sense that you may have an out-of-body experience. The forces and the other souls you encounter may include some that would hinder and divert your best spiritual growth. There are influences that can be troublesome for you, and so preparation is prudent whenever possible.

Cayce usually recommended that people imagine themselves surrounded by light or the universal Christ consciousness as a protection. For example, one woman asked in her reading if she should allow herself to go out of her body. The response was affirmative, with one important qualification: *if and when* she had learned how to surround herself with the influence of the Christ consciousness to prevent being misled by hindering forces.

6. *You may hear an unusual noise in your head just before an out-of-body experience.* It may sound like the waves of the ocean, the wind blowing, or a buzzing. Cayce explained "the increase of the noise" to one man as "the raising of that vibration that exists between . . . the material and the spiritual" (no. 900–328). If you hear something like this as you are falling asleep, don't be alarmed.

7. *If you find yourself in the midst of an astral projection or a lucid dream, there is one principal rule to follow: act on your ideals.* Try to do something that reflects your highest values. These higher worlds are places of reality just like the physical world. What you think, feel, and do has meaning and impact.

One astral projectionist asked in his Cayce reading: "For what purpose do I leave my body, and how can I develop this power con-- structively?" We can all apply and benefit from the response he received. Cayce told him first to clarify his desires. What was he looking for? What did he seek in his spiritual development? Next, he was warned against viewing these astral trips as amazing performances. Finally, he was instructed with these words to act out his highest ideals whenever he found himself out of the physical body: "Study to show thyself approved unto God, a workman not ashamed of that you think, of that you do, or of your acts; keeping self unspotted from your own . . . ideal" (no. 853–8).

CONTACTING THE DECEASED AT AN ASTRAL LEVEL

What about communicating with the dead while at an astral level? In chapter eight we looked at evidence suggesting that some of our dreams about deceased individuals may be direct soul-to-soul contacts. Is the same thing possible during out-of-body experiences into astral dimensions? The Cayce readings clearly indicated that this may happen, but warnings and important details were added.

First, we must remember that the astral plane is not the highest reality. It is a dimension of consciousness that we may visit briefly at night; and it is a level to which the soul goes for some period of time after death. But it is not the ultimate goal. It is not "heaven." There are higher dimensions of the spiritual world.

Second, we should keep in mind that within the astral world there are many levels of vibration. It is analogous to the physical world. Here in the material plane there are many different kinds of people, and a great diversity of spiritual development. Similarly, there are lower and higher states of development within the astral world. Some souls in the astral plane are confused and misled, others are wise and helpful. If and when we make contact with another soul in an astral dimension, we must be discerning.

If you encounter another soul during an astral projection or a lucid dream, what might you experience? If you get information or guidance, evaluate it upon awakening, just as you would any advice. Does it resonate to your highest values? Is this guidance consistent with your own ideals? If not, then ignore what you have received from the astral encounter. Don't follow guidance just because it came from an unusual source.

Not every humanlike form you encounter during an astral experience is necessarily an active soul. For example, Cayce interpreted an interesting out-of-body experience in which a woman met "people who seemed like waxen images of themselves." He said that they were astral shells left behind when the souls had moved on into higher spiritual worlds.

In that same experience the woman saw her deceased father and his two brothers. They did not look like these astral shells, but instead seemed animated and active. The unusual feature in their appearance was their age. Rather than looking like white-haired old men, as she remembered them just before their deaths, they looked like young men. Cayce's interpretation was that we can expect to see this age change in a soul at the astral plane whenever the soul is learning and growing once again.

Many other examples are given in the Cayce readings of astral contacts with departed relatives. One of the most fascinating stories concerns a young woman whose mother had recently died. In an astral-level experience she heard the voice of an old friend who had died three weeks earlier. The voice said that she had been present to help the mother with her transition into the afterlife. It reassured the young woman with the words: "Your mother is as happy as ever."

The Cayce reading confirmed the validity of this astral experience. The old friend had really been present to assist with the mother's passing. The friendship and companionship between the two had survived bodily death.

Then the young woman asked, "Does my mother see me and love me as ever?" The reading promised that loved ones who have passed on are still mindful of those left behind, and that contact is possible whenever the one still in a physical body makes the right attunement.

This is an exciting and hopeful promise to anyone bereaved by the loss of a friend or family member. But it is tempered by statements made in other Cayce readings that warn against preoccupation with astral contacts. Apparently, if we pursue this too often, it can cause distress for the soul that has moved on. Too great a focus on trying to create astral-level reunions can hold back the loved one from necessary experiences on the other side. The best advice, therefore, is this: stay alert and open for such an encounter, but let the soul that has passed on take the initiative.

UNDERSTANDING DREAMS OF POWER

The experiences we have examined in this chapter are some of the most extraordinary available to us during sleep. We might well call them dreams of power for two reasons.

First, such experiences almost invariably convey to the dreamer in waking life a spiritual power. They are spiritually revitalizing. An astral projection, out-of-body experience, or lucid dream can leave the individual filled with an exhilarating potency that carries over into daily living.

Second, in these experiences we discover something of our own creative, spiritual powers. We see directly that we are citizens of an immense universe that extends not just to the far reaches of outer space, but to the limitless potentials of inner space.

Lest we misunderstand what these dreams of power come to teach us, let's remember this fundamental law of spiritual growth: *everything we seek can be found within.* Even the astral dimension is within ourselves. Our objective should not be to see how far out of the body we can go. Instead, it is to see how much love and wisdom we can bring into the body.

And so, the greatest astral trip might well be the one that ventures most deeply into inner space. This was exactly the lesson learned by a contemporary dreamer who had frequent out-of-body experiences. After considerable study of this phenomenon, he decided that the next time it happened to him, he would respond in a new way: he would pray during the astral projection.

It didn't take long for him to have the opportunity. Soon thereafter he had a dream in which he felt himself leaving his body. In this case it was his astral body projecting out of his dream body. As he sensed the separation taking place, he began to pray fervently, "God, take me to the place where I most need to be." Immediately, he felt himself sucked right back into his dream body. But the dream continued, and now he was lucid. What followed was the most beautiful and inspiring lucid dream he had ever had—one in which he felt the unseen presence of Jesus.

The conclusion he reached in analyzing this remarkable dream is relevant for us all. His tendency had always been to think that a spiritual experience requires going off somewhere—to Tibet, to the Great Pyramid, or to a distant location on the astral plane. This lucid dream had shown him the presence of God within himself.

10

ESP and Dream Guidance

Psychic is of the soul. This simple principle is found time and again in Cayce readings that explain how ESP—extrasensory perception—works.

Psychic ability is possible because you are a soul—a spiritual being. Experiences of ESP are direct, personal evidence of this invisible reality. How have you already caught a glimpse of your soul-self in action? Was it a hunch about someone that proved to be true? An intuitive insight that seemed to come out of nowhere but solved a troublesome problem? An inner sense of warning that kept you from some kind of harm?

These are just a few of the ways that you may have already experienced your own psychic potential. But the greatest area of possibility is with your dreams. For many people the easiest way to have a psychic experience is during sleep. With great frequency your dreams are psychic. They allow you to tune in to the thoughts and feelings of others (telepathy), they look into the future to warn or to offer promises (precognition), and they look back into the forgotten past, maybe even to previous lifetimes (retrocognition).

In this chapter we will explore each of these types of psychic dreaming. And, since psychic dreaming is so closely tied to the topic of receiving guidance, we will examine a strategy offered by the Cayce readings for how to get a psychic guidance dream.

DREAM TELEPATHY

Louise, a woman in her mid-thirties, had recorded and studied her dreams for several years. She had already discovered many of the practical ways in which her dreams could help her with daily life issues. But one night she had a dream that puzzled her afterward, because she could see no place where it fit her waking life:

> My husband and I are driving along a familiar road when we spot a church. I ask him to stop because I know that my grade school is having a reunion there, and I might see friends from twenty-five years ago.
> We go in, but I see no one I recognize. We're about to leave when I spot my friend Peggy. It is a thrill to see her, and we are both overjoyed to renew our friendship. We hug and talk until the dream ends.

The approaches to interpretation Louise normally used were not productive for this dream. She decided to put it aside, thinking that she might get insights about it later. Five days afterward she unexpectedly discovered that this had been a telepathic dream. She received a letter from her mother with some amazing news. The very day that Louise had had the dream, her mother ran into Peggy in a shopping mall. None of the family had seen or heard from Peggy for years, so Louise's mother got all the details of what had been happening in Peggy's life and included them in the letter.

This was a dramtic instance of dream telepathy. Louise had not been thinking about this childhood friend, and yet the very day she was found by her mother, Louise picked up on their reunion in a dream.

Compare that story to another one from the Cayce readings. A twenty-two-year-old woman dreamed that her friend Emmie committed suicide. Edgar Cayce's analysis of this experience described it as a literal mind-to-mind communication. Emmie had been thinking about committing suicide. The thoughts had since passed, but the dream had occurred during the period when suicide was contemplated.

The dreamer asked two follow-up questions in the reading. First, "Will Emmie kill herself?" The response was that this telepathic dream only tuned in on thoughts that Emmie was entertaining. It was not predictive of an actual suicide.

Second, the dreamer wondered, "How did this information about Emmie get into my dream life?" The answer pointed to two key facts about the human mind: Thoughts are things, and Emmie's contemplation of suicide had created an idea animated by spiritual energy. Furthermore, all subconscious minds are in contact with each other. A link—a bridge—at the mental level connects us to each other. When we sleep and dream at night, the subconscious mind comes more fully into our awareness and makes telepathic dreaming not only possible but likely.

When we compare the stories of Louise and the young woman who received a Cayce reading, we are struck by their difference. Of course, both telepathic dreams demonstrate how thoughts are things and how subconscious minds are connected. But the first story was more trivial—an interesting curiosity. The second story was a matter of life and death. You will probably discover the same contrast among your own telepathic dreams. Some of them seem to come for playful reasons. Perhaps they are merely to remind you of your psychic potential and to show you again how people really *are* connected at unseen levels. Other telepathic dreams bring you vital information— facts you need in order to love and help others. They are the dreams you don't want to miss.

Of course not all telepathic dreams can be taken at face value. Some are genuine psychic contacts, but the events of the dream are symbolic. For example:

> My wife sneaks up behind me and repeatedly hits me on my head with a broom handle. As she is hitting me she yells, "February!"

This dream bewildered him for two reasons: he and his wife seemed to be getting along well; and it was the middle of the summer and not February. But as he carefully considered possible interpretations, he decided to pursue the chance that it might be telepathic. He told the dream to his wife and was surprised to learn that it concerned her unspoken feelings. She had strong, hurt feelings from an argument in February and she was still mad at him about those events.

The same man proved to be a telepathic dreamer on another occasion, again with events best understood as symbolic rather than literal. A new female employee at his place of work seemed to be a pleasant person, although a bit overwhelmed by her new position with the company. But even though he had noticed her, he was too busy to get to know her. To his dismay he woke up one morning with an unlikely dream in which he had started a romantic relationship with this woman. The dream included a passionate lovemaking scene.

He was rather embarrassed by the dream and told no one of it. He couldn't see how or why he should have had such an experience—in his waking state he felt no particular attraction to her. But, months later, as they slowly became good friends, he discovered the telepathic quality of the dream. At one point she admitted that during her early weeks on the job, she had deeply felt the need for a sympathetic colleague. The new job had proved to be difficult and she wanted an ally during this hard period. His telepathic dream had picked up on her thoughts and needs, and it had presented them symbolically as "intimacy." Fortunately, he had not taken this to be guidance to pursue a sexual encounter. In fact, their relationship remained a close friendship and never took a romantic turn.

Romantic relationships, or any that have strong emotional bonds, are a prime area for telepathic dreaming. We tend to dream about the things that concern us most, and love relationships are likely to be high on our lists. But even when a dream proves to be telepathic, we cannot assume that *everthing* in that dream is genuinely psychic. This important point is illustrated by a great misunderstanding created by one dreamer's psychic experience.

Greg and Cindy, both college students, were lovers. When Thanksgiving came Greg went home to visit his family. Cindy stayed behind to catch up on studies. A day after Greg departed Cindy's former boyfriend, Bill, came to town unexpectedly. He had been living more than a thousand miles away, and no one had heard from him for a long time. But Bill knew that Cindy was going to college in this particular town, and he called her as he was passing through. They agreed to get together.

At his parents' home Greg had a troubling dream in which Cindy had dropped their relationship and renewed a romance with her old boyfriend. He woke up quite upset, but as he thought about it later he could see no reason why he would have had such a dream. Imagine his feelings when he called Cindy and learned that Bill was visiting that very day!

He assumed that since the dream psychically picked up on the *outer event* of Bill's surprising arrival, then it must also be accurate about the *inner event* of Cindy's changing affections. However, such was not the case. Although it took some time for him to be convinced, no love relation was rekindled by Cindy and Bill's reunion. That aspect of the dream was *not* psychically correct.

How could such a dream happen? By what process could a dream be such a mixture of accurate and inaccurate material? Remember, the Cayce readings stated that all subconscious minds are in contact with each other. However, the readings also suggested that psychic information coming into conscious awareness must pass through the subconscious mind of the recipient. This can be illustrated by the following diagram:

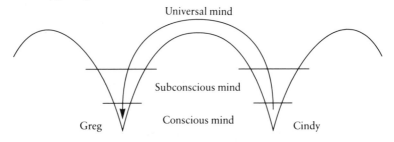

Suppose that the arrow represents information about Cindy's life that is available to Greg in his dreams. As it passes through his own subconscious mind it may be distorted. His own fears and insecurities may be added in. This is exactly what happened. Greg was later able to appreciate how his own lack of confidence created part of this telepathic dream.

This story and the preceding ones show us several important things to keep in mind. Mind-to-mind communication through dreams actually occurs, perhaps quite frequently. But even when we get confirming evidence that a dream is psychic, we must still be alert for symbolic rather than literal meanings. In addition, we must refrain from jumping to the conclusion that everything about the dream is necessarily accurate. With those precautions in mind dreams can be a valuable way for us to get insights about people and relationships.

PRECOGNITION: DREAMS OF THE FUTURE

Once Edgar Cayce's wife, Gertrude, asked for a reading to interpret one of her own dreams. The dream involved action with both Edgar and herself as key figures in the story, and it proved to be a look into the future. But before a specific interpretation was offered, the reading gave a general description of how precognitive dreams are possible.

The reading asked Gertrude (and any of us today who are interested in psychic dreaming) to imagine this scene. A man is walking from Virginia Beach, Virginia, westward toward Norfolk, which is about fifteen miles away. He can we know that the individual will actually reach Norfolk? With what reliability can we foresee the outcome of this journey? The best that can be said is that, if conditions stay the same, the outcome is predictable. If the traveler stays on the road and keeps walking he will eventually reach Norfolk.

Admittedly, this analogy is simplistic. Yet it makes a profound point about what can and cannot be known psychically about the future. Since the future is not fixed, no psychic or precognitive dream can say for certain that something specific will happen. However, it *is* possible to be sensitive to what will happen *if* things follow their current pathway. The reading for Gertrude put it this way: "an individual on . . . a certain trend of mind is certain to reach a definite position" (no. 538–25). At any given moment in life you have a specific trend of mind—attitudes, feelings, and tentative decisions you are leaning toward making. If you stay with those trends then where you will end up is fairly predictable. You may not be able to see the likely future with your *conscious mind*, but the bigger perspective of your dreams can.

Cayce's interpretations pointed to two different purposes of precognitive dreams. Most important is *to give feedback* on the current trend of things in your life. Sometimes that feedback is to confirm a positive trend by showing you in a dream the good results that are likely for the future. More often, though, the feedback is useful because it gives a warning. Precognitive dreams can caution that the future you are now choosing and creating is not one that will make you happy.

The second purpose of precognitive dreams is simply *to provide useful information*. A part of your subconscious mind is always looking ahead. It is not trying to judge whether or not you are on the right road, but merely to notice events and situations that are likely to occur. Here are some examples that show how this kind of dream may look.

Robert's Dream

Robert rarely had the chance to see Rebecca, his friend from college years. They lived in different cities and were both very happy but busy with careers and families. Each of them had chosen a vocation as a counselor, and so they still had much in common. On those infrequent occasions when they would see each other, they still felt a close bond of friendship. But their hectic, demanding lifestyles got in the way of anything more.

One night Robert dreamed about Rebecca. The two of them, with their respective children, were all dancing in a circle together. The dream was filled with joy and celebration. However, upon awakening, he noticed one unusual feature of this dream: the children all appeared to be three or four years older than they really were at the time.

At first Robert paid it little attention, thinking it to be simply a wish-fulfillment dream—a product of his occasional desire to see more of his longtime friend. Or, he thought, perhaps the symbol of Rebecca represented some aspect of his own personality with which he was getting in better touch.

Only as he looked back in his dream journal years later did he see that this had been a psychic dream. It had accurately predicted certain events that came to pass after four years. As the children grew older, both Robert and Rebecca found that they had more time to invest in their careers. They both independently formed an intention to begin to write and to try to get an article published in a professional counseling journal. When they next met and discovered they had similar plans, they decided to collaborate. The result was a series of three published articles over a period of several years.

The precognitive dream had come true. The clue to its real meaning had been hidden in the curious feature of the children's ages. In fact, this is a quality of many precognitive dreams, and it may help you recognize your own at the time the dream comes. Look for some unusual aspect of *timing*: clock or dates moved ahead, friends or family members who look older, and so forth. This signpost won't be in every dream about the future, but it may allow you to recognize some of them.

Wendy's Dream

Other precognitive dreams may be so mysterious that when they come it is almost impossible to recognize them for what they are. Valuable information may be provided, but its helpfulness cannot be appreciated immediately. This is one of the best reasons to write down your dreams daily. When you keep a journal of your experiences you can periodically look back and see if any old dreams are starting to make sense in light of new situations.

For example, Wendy and her husband moved from the West Coast to the East Coast without having yet sold their house. Because the move needed to happen right away, she left the sale of the house in the hands of her sister. Wendy was worried about how quickly it might sell.

In the midst of this time of worry she had a curious dream:

I am sitting at a table with my sister and two other people: a
Vietnamese woman and a strange man. Apparently the woman is newly
married, and I say to her, "I hope I don't offend you, but isn't being

newly married hard enough without adding the problem of language and money differences?" Then I wake up.

Nothing in that dream would easily have shown Wendy its precognitive nature, yet it was giving her information that later proved to be valuable. Two months after the dream, Wendy got a call from her sister and learned that a couple was very interested in the house. The man was a Navy officer and his wife was Vietnamese. At that point Wendy remembered her dream about the Vietnamese woman—a dream that had come right at the height of her worries about the house. The couple eventually bought the house.

Instructive and Warning Dreams

There are also numerous examples of predictive dreams in the Cayce interpretations. Many of them illustrate the activities of a special part of the mind, one that seems to be always looking ahead, alert for new situations that are likely to arise.

In one case an eighteen-year-old boy dreamed about rather ordinary circumstances: "My parents decide to leave home and I'm left in charge of the house. No sooner have they departed than visitors arrive unexpectedly." The interpretation offered in the reading was straightforward. These events were likely to happen in a literal way. His parents would probably take a trip soon and leave him in charge, but he should be prepared for company to come. The purpose of the dream was to provide him with information that would be useful.

Cayce's interpretations more often emphasized the other purpose of precognitive dreams, which was to give feedback about the current trend. That feedback is often in the form of a *warning*.

One of the most dramatic examples concerns an inventor in his mid-forties. He and others were working on the development of new engineering principles for a motor. In the midst of this creative time he dreamed that he was working on the motor and his shirt was dirty. He left to change his shirt, but when he came back the automobile and its new motor had been stolen. The dream ended with his thought of dismay, "It was taken right in front of my face."

In a reading to decipher this dream Cayce stated that it was a precognitive warning. The current trend of his life made it likely that "through the littleness of others" his creative efforts would be stolen from him. But there was still hope; things did not have to go that way. It was within his power to change the course of things, but not merely by taking security precautions out of fear. Instead, the recommendation was to watch his own attitudes and ideals carefully in regard to the motor. The fact that he wore a dirty shirt in the dream indicated a "soiled" or improper attitude on his own part. If that trend continued it would make him vulnerable to other people with selfish, greedy intent. But if he would remind himself of his highest purpose for the invention and stay focused on it, then he need not fear.

A second example of precognitive warning can be found in the dream of a newlywed woman. Her dream was simple but disturbing: she got into a quarrel with her new mother-in-law. Cayce's interpretation described its predictive quality. There was a trend of mind within the two of them that would likely lead to a dispute. If things had been allowed to stay on their current course a quarrel was inevitable. He counseled the young woman to make those changes within herself that would alter the conditions—she could act to prevent this occurrence. She was clearly reminded by the Cayce reading—as we all should be—that the future is not fixed. Even the most insightful precognitive dream shows us events that are still in the process of being created.

RETROCOGNITION: PAST-LIFE DREAMS

The psychic side of dreaming is controversial. Not every dream theory agrees with Cayce's notion that ESP is frequently present in dreams. But perhaps even more controversial is the subject of reincarnation—the idea that we have all had previous human lives which largely shape our current life situation. The readings of Edgar Cayce strongly support this position, and even suggest that some of our dreams include recall of past lives. This kind of psychic dreaming we might call retrocognitive.

You need not believe in reincarnation to follow the Cayce approach to dream study. However, an open-minded willingness to entertain the *possibility* may help you see meaning to dreams that would otherwise be baffling. If the idea of reincarnation is new to you, it is worthwhile to do some reading in other books that explain the theory and how it works.

Occasionally, a dream will bluntly present a past life. For example:

> While driving on a busy city street I suddenly lose control of my car and hit the auto in front of me. I am thrown forward into the windshield. At impact I seem to go out of my physical body and travel up into the clouds, where I find myself standing in front of what seems like a huge library. I cautiously go in and find hundreds of shelves of books. Each book is lettered on the spine with the name of an individual, and after some searching I discover a book with my name.
>
> I open the book and begin to read about myself. First I read the story of a past life in which I had been a student and coworker with the famous scientist Galileo. Then, as I begin to read about another past life, I seem to enter into the story and experience it directly. I see myself as a rather well-to-do landowner. From the appearance of my home and the dress of the people, it looks like the early nineteenth century in America. I am standing in my drawing room, and just across the room I see a woman whom I know to be my wife. I immediately feel our mutual love and common interests. Her appearance is unfamiliar, but as I look into her eyes I know it is the same soul as one I love in my current twentieth-century lifetime. Then the scene fades and I wake up.

Clearly, this seemed to have been two past-life recall experiences in a single dream. But why would such memories have come to him? Although Edgar Cayce was unavailable to give a reading on this dream, there is a Cayce principle about past-life dreams that would help this man see its purpose. *Past-life dreams come, not to satisfy curiosity, but to help us deal with challenges and opportunities in the present.*

When the man looked at his remarkable dream in this light, he saw just how helpful it was. The first part of the dream helped him understand a dilemma about his vocation. Since childhood he had felt drawn to the sciences, and yet his career path had gone in a different direction. Although things were going well for him in his work, he still felt a nagging doubt. Had he made the wrong choice? This dream allowed him to put these worries to rest. His lifelong pull to science was a soul memory. He might well have developed talents in that past life which were to be used in the present one, but he need not feel constrained to repeat something he had already done skillfully hundreds of years ago.

The second part of the dream was equally relevant to another current problem. He had a close relationship with a woman in this lifetime, but prospects for marriage looked dim. Many things were right between the two of them, but various obstacles came up whenever they considered marriage. It was as if they weren't destined to be together permanently in this lifetime. Although she had a different appearance in the nineteenth-century lifetime of the dream, he knew that this was the same soul.

This past-life dream helped the man see that he was trying to recreate something that the two of them had already had. It was quite natural for them to be attracted to each other, and even to consider marriage. But he now saw that the obstacles that continually arose were guidance signs. As souls they had chosen different plans for this experience. The dream helped him attain peace of mind about the situation. He was able to release the relationship and to let a genuine and deep friendship remain without forcing a past-life memory to repeat itself.

Another example shows again that some past-life dreams depict the memory in literal form. In this case the dream came to help explain a fear that had been present since early childhood. The dreamer was a woman in her late thirties:

> I am in a business meeting where my boss is jokingly telling others about a past life that he and I had had together. As I listen I begin to remember yet another lifetime and move into that scene.
>
> I am about five or six years old, living on a farm with my older sister and my mother. My father is away as a soldier in a war. I know that I am very intelligent for my age and can speak at least one other

language. I irritate my sister whenver I talk in that foreign language to our farm workers, because she doesn't know what we're discussing.

Then I look up and see on the horizon a band of soldiers riding on horseback toward us. They are wearing metallic, bowl-shaped helmets, baggy pants, and mail vests. They are big and ferocious, and everyone on the farm is trying to find a place to hide. I have a music box in my hand and I take it with me as I hide in a closet full of clothes and junk. But I can't get the music box to stop playing its tune. I would probably have been overlooked by the invaders, but the music box gives me away and I'm caught by one of the soldiers. Then I wake up.

The dream allowed her to understand her irrational fear of going into a closet. As a child she felt a queasiness in her stomach when playing "hide and seek," and she could never quite bring herself to try hiding in a closet. But as a child, and even now as an adult, she was very fond of music boxes. This past-life recall through a dream helped her release her anxieties. She now understood where the fear had begun, and it ceased to be a problem for her.

The same woman had another past-life dream that permitted her to see a new side of interpersonal relationships. She and her husband were acting as temporary foster parents in their community. Children would come to live with them who were victims of child abuse or disrupted homes. They were especially fond of one family's four children who had come to live with them on two occasions. The woman often wondered why she felt so close to these four youngsters.

One night she had a dream that answered her question. Although none of the characters resembled the favorite foster children, she woke from it sure that it was a past-life memory about them:

I am a child living in medieval times. My young brother and I like to play in the village on the main road to the castle. We stop playing when we see two familiar young women walk by. As we wave to the women, two young men ride up on horseback. They are obviously interested in showing off for these two ladies they admire.

My brother and I call to the horsemen by name, and they ride over to us. Playfully, they scoop us up and put us on the saddles in front of them. This is not the first time we have played this game, and we love to go riding this way.

When she woke from the dream, she had a strong intuition that it concerned the four foster children. Her feeling was that the young brother was her current husband, and that the two pairs of young men and women were now the four children. The special place in her heart for those four began to make more sense to her. She saw that a reciprocal feeling of taking care of each other was perfectly logical in light of reincarnation.

Edgar Cayce's dream interpretations sometimes referred to reincarnation. One woman had recurrent dreams in which she wandered through a large temple looking for someone. Sometimes flames in the temple blocked her way; sometimes she got lost in a crowd. Her reading described this as a reincarnation memory, from a lifetime in ancient Egypt. The scenes from the recurrent dream related to difficult times she had with spiritual and political authority.

Edgar Cayce himself sometimes had past-life dreams. One example is especially noteworthy because it shows that not all reincarnation dreams necessarily look that way at first. Sometimes the past-life quality of a dream can be clothed in modern-day images.

When he was fifty years old Cayce dreamed of a female friend from his present lifetime. The two of them were in a scene with some rather rough men, one of whom captured the woman. He held her in such a way to protect himself so that no one would try to shoot him. Cayce the dreamer came to the rescue. He got a gun and shot the man through the foot. The bullet traveled magically up through his body, down his arm, and out through his hand, causing the man to drop his gun. The woman was able to escape.

A reading given to interpret this dream said that it was a past-life memory depicted in modern images. As souls in a different lifetime, Cayce and this woman had been together on the American frontier of the nineteenth century. She had been his companion in a daring escape from a besieged fort. Within Cayce's own soul memory there was an impulse to be protective of this person. The reading encouraged him to develop this function in their present relationship, but to broaden it so that it encompassed protective help for physical, mental, and spiritual concerns.

Not all reincarnation dreams appear in the costumes and settings of the distant past, so we must be alert for the little clues that might tip us off to a past-life memory. The dream may include a pun that refers to another incarnation. For example: French doors, Chinese food, or a Japanese garden. Sometimes the clue may be a single symbol. A tomahawk could represent a Native American lifetime; or a camel might symbolize an incarnation living in the desert. We can never be sure from just one image that the dream is past-life retrocognition—a tomahawk or a camel could both have many other possible meanings.

But as we look for clues they may suggest interpretations that refer to the distant past. Those references come to assist us. They show how the thoughts, emotions, and deeds of long ago may still be active within our souls. One Cayce reading puts it this way: "For to the subconscious [that is, the source of dreams] there is no past or future—all present" (no. 136–54). Even though the Renaissance period or the Crusades or ancient Egypt may sound far off in time to us, it really isn't. If reincarnation is, in fact, the truth of how souls grow, then dreams occasionally show us just how alive those influences still are.

GUIDANCE FROM YOUR DREAMS

Life can be confusing. Contradictory signs and influences abound in the world around us. So when we face an important decision, what do we do? How do we go about finding a reliable answer?

Our dreams can have a significant role to play. They won't be the only thing on which we rely, but dreams will be an invaluable friend and counselor. Ultimately, *we* will have to make the decision, but during sleep we can get extra information and direction.

Everything in this book concerns dream guidance. That's what dream study is all about. Every night we get feedback on these general questions: Who am I? What is my life all about? What do I need to change so that I will be happier?

In this section, however, we will explore a more specific approach to dream guidance: how to get help dealing with a particular problem. Your dreams will provide assistance when you face a decision concerning health, finances, relationships, career, and almost anything else. You can follow practical steps to get the best your dreams have to offer.

It is important to understand that dreams should not make decisions *for you*. They will work *with you*, but a key aspect of spiritual growth is learning how to make loving, productive decisions that benefit yourself and others. In the long run it is irresponsible and immature to blame your decisions on dreams. You can well imagine how frustrating it can be to hear someone say, "Well, if things didn't turn out right, that's too bad. But I was just doing what my dreams told me to do." This kind of attitude tries to stay removed from the decision-making process and responsibility.

From one point of view it might be said that the best example of a guidance dream given in this book appeared in chapter eight, in the section on Peak Spiritual Experiences (page 99). It was the dream of a woman who faced a career decision and dreamed that the Virgin Mary came to her to help. The dreamer was led to a psychic whom the Virgin Mary promised was a highly reliable source of direction. But the psychic offered support only by reaffirming that the dreamer was capable of making a good decision for herself. She woke feeling more self-confident, prepared to use her own intuition and common sense to make her choice.

Naturally you may sometimes want something more than what this woman received. More detailed information or direction is often useful. Not only can you trust that such help will come, but you can take certain steps to prepare for such a dream. It is a matter of doing your "homework" so that when the "teacher" arrives (that is, your dreams) the most learning can take place. It is like preparing the soil of your garden bed before you plant seeds, so that the strongest, most productive plants will grow.

The process of getting ready to receive a guidance dream is called *dream incubation*. It has been practiced for centuries, going back at least to ancient Greece, where people traveled to dream temples in order to get a guidance dream. Usually the questions they wanted answered were about physical health. The preparatory procedures in the temple were designed to invite the Greek god of healing, Aesculapius, to appear in the dream, give a psychic diagnosis, and recommend a treatment regimen.

You can follow similar steps in today's world, and your question need *not* be limited to health issues. You can make your own bedroom into a "dream guidance temple." The keys are to get yourself prepared to receive the inner direction and to stay open-minded concerning what may come.

A good way to get started is to do some writing in your dream journal right before you go to bed. This activity helps to focus your energies and it starts to act as a suggestive influence to your subconscious mind. One format is to answer six questions. They represent some of the best ideas of the Cayce readings and the pioneering work in dream guidance by researchers Gayle Delaney, Henry Reed, and Robert Van de Castle.

1. In what area of my life do I feel a need to get an answer to a problem, concern, or difficulty?

2. What exactly is it that I want to know? (Word your question carefully and precisely.)

3. Being totally honest with myself, are there any benefits or advantages that I get from *not* having this question resolved? (Examples: sympathy from others, excuses, financial rewards, and so forth.)

4. What information have I gathered so far concerning an answer to my question? (List the factors or pieces of the puzzle that you have knowledge of at this point.)

5. What is the best answer that I can *consciously* formulate right now to my question, before I go to sleep and dream? (You may feel that this tentative answer lacks some wisdom or insight, but do the best you can as a preliminary effort.)

6. What question do I want answered? (Write a short sleep suggestion that you can use tonight—a *brief statement of the question* which you can focus on as you drift off to sleep.)

Once you have finished your journal writing, go to bed. Make sure that you have paper and pen close at hand so that you can write down upon awakening *any* dreams you recall. (Don't be too quick to dismiss a dream as irrelevant to your question.) As you feel yourself relaxing and beginning to drift off, silently repeat in your mind the sleep suggestion that you composed earlier. It need not be the last thing you have on your mind before falling asleep. What counts is that you really desire an answer to your question. Repeating your suggestion by rote and without emotion won't work. Say the suggestion to yourself—silently or aloud—and *feel* how you truly mean it.

Finally, let the whole thing go. Release any concerns about the success or failure of this experiment. Many people have discovered a tendency to worry all night long whether or not the dream guidance has come. That is the surest way to block the process. Just let it go. You have done your part, now allow your dreams to do theirs.

When you awaken in the morning write down all the dreams (or fragments) that you can remember. Don't be selective—you may not be wise enough at first to see what is and isn't important to your question.

Once you have the dreams recorded in your journal you can begin to interpret them. Use any and all the techniques described in this book, but especially be alert for one of the following four possibilities. These are the types of experience that come most often when people incubate a dream for guidance:

1. The dream *restates* the question from a new point of view. It doesn't answer the question but instead gives you new information about it. By looking at the problem from a different perspective it may allow you to see an answer for yourself.

2. The dream is *predictive*: It shows what is likely to happen in that part of your life *if* you follow the momentum of your current tendencies (the tentative decision you wrote down as step 5 in the journal exercise). Based on what the predictive dream shows, you can decide whether or not those are the results you are hoping for. If not, then the guidance is to go back and change your tentative decision.

3. The dream proposes an *exact answer* or solution to your question. This is the kind of dream that most people hope to get because it is direct. You may find that you, the dreamer, or some other dream character is acting out the solution. Or some person in your dream may offer advice that is relevant to your problem.

4. The dream does not address your stated question. Instead, it calls attention to *another question* that must be resolved first. Sometimes there are "questions behind our questions," and good solutions can be found only if we take the questions in the proper order. Your dream incubation question is probably a good one, and your dream life is not trying to avoid the problem but rather deal with it in due time. You must deal with the preliminary question before your original question can be addressed.

It is especially because of the fourth type of dream that you should not prematurely dismiss a dream as irrelevant. At face value it may appear to have nothing to do with the people or situations dealing with your primary question, but such a dream may be useful and important. For example, if your question concerns a vocational decision, your dream may speak first about your level of self-confidence. Until you resolve that issue, you may not be able to make the decision on career that is in your best interest. Or, if your question concerns what medicines to take in order to get well, your guidance dream may first point to different issues. What is your attitude toward your body? For what purposes do you want to be healthy? Those questions should be resolved first.

No matter which of the four types of dream you seem to get, there comes a point where you must evaluate the guidance. You shouldn't just follow the interpretation blindly. It's unwise to act *solely* because the guidance came from a dream. Ask yourself, "Is this good advice? Is this high-quality guidance?" Evaluate what you have received in light of the following nine criteria. If it is reliable spiritual guidance, then you should be able to affirm most or all of these features.

1. Does this guidance have the "ring of truth" to it?
2. Does it fit with the *best* that I know I should be doing, not just something acceptable?
3. Does it help me see things beyond my conscious understanding? Does it stretch me to see things in a new way?
4. Does the guidance seem reasonable?
5. In the dream, who is presenting the guidance? Is that the sort of person in waking life whom I would trust?
6. Does the guidance leave me feeling hopeful about my life?
7. If I apply the guidance, can I expect to see benefits coming to me and to *all* others involved?
8. Would following this guidance give me peace of mind?
9. Does a trusted close friend agree with my interpretation?

Now, with this program for dream incubation clearly in mind, you are ready to get started. Getting guidance from your dreams is quite an adventure. Tools like the simple story line or the Cayce Dream Symbol Dictionary are just stepping stones for discovering how practical and helpful dreams can be. The messages in your dreams concern the spoken and unspoken questions with which you wrestle each day. Dream incubation is simply a focused, direct way to cooperate with this natural, ongoing process.

Incubating a guidance dream is also the best way to experience the psychic side of dreaming. Remember that Cayce always defined "psychic" in the broadest way: it pertains to the soul or spiritual forces. To assist you with your question, your dream life may sometimes have to draw upon telepathic abilities. Other times it may require precognitive dreaming or retrocognitive looks at past-life influences. But the purpose of psychic dream guidance is always the same: to provide messages from your inner self that help you live more happily and productively.

PART IV

The Edgar Cayce Dream Symbol Dictionary

THE EDGAR CAYCE DREAM SYMBOL DICTIONARY is like none other that you will find. Like any other dictionary, it has an array of possible meanings for many common symbols. But it also has a *synopsis of each dream* in which the symbol appears. In other words, you get to see the *context* in which the symbol fits into a larger dream experience.

Generally speaking, dream dictionaries are not designed to be read cover to cover. They are for reference only. However, *this* dictionary is fun to read, because the dreams themselves are included. You can have a valuable learning experience about symbol interpretation by studying this part of the book.

Here is one way to make an instructive game of it. Pick a symbol from among the ones listed in the dictionary. Try reading the dream synopses *before* you look just above them to see how Cayce interpreted the symbol in question. Sometimes you may find that you would have interpreted the symbol just the way he did. In other instances it will be harder to see how he logically arrived at the symbol meaning that is listed. But remember that often Cayce was drawing upon his own psychic sensitivity to the deeper mind of the dreamer.

The Cayce Dream Symbol Dictionary can be an extraordinary resource to you for personal dream study. It contains all the specific symbol interpretations in the hundreds of dreams that were deciphered by Cayce.

This dictionary includes more than two hundred symbols. Most symbols appeared in several dreams, so Cayce has offered more than one possible meaning. Of course, these meanings are not the only possible ones. Use the dictionary as a way of getting started, as a resource to get your own creative insights flowing.

For most entries in the dictionary you will also find a subsection entitled "Other possibilities." Here you will find additional meanings that a symbol could have, even though it was never interpreted that way in a Cayce reading.

Occasionally, a symbol is listed as a subheading to a large category. For example, "eagle" is listed under "BIRD: eagle." In addition, some symbols are interpreted by Cayce in a particular way because of their specific characteristics. For example, "teeth" may mean one thing, but "false teeth" something different. Frequently you will find in the dictionary that multiple meanings are listed for a symbol, but that several of the options are for a specialized version of that symbolic image.

As you use the Cayce Dream Symbol Dictionary, you will discover that certain symbols are especially rich in possible meanings, whereas for other symbols only one or two meanings are listed. Be sure to use the techniques described in chapter seven to uncover your own, personalized associations with a particular symbol. In that chapter there are three approaches for creatively interpreting a dream symbol.

Take a moment to glance through the dictionary. Get a feeling for its layout and how you might use it. Try looking at a couple of symbols in detail. For example, you might pick "DEATH," a symbol that Cayce interpreted often and which can deeply disturb us if we don't know how to interpret it. Cayce readings described the meaning of this symbol in ten different ways. All the most *common* meanings are covered, so there is no need for a section called "Other possibilities." Nevertheless, you might possibly have a dream in which death has an uncommon interpretation. Using the three approaches described in chapter seven, you would be able to discover some other, more personal meaning for this symbol.

You will notice in the entries for DEATH that some are for specialized versions. The fourth interpretation is for the death of a brother; the seventh interpretation is for one's own after-death state of consciousness.

Next, look at the entry for DIAMOND. Cayce interpreted this symbol in only one dream, but there are at least six other common meanings for you to consider.

Think of the symbol dictionary in this book as a starting point for your own dictionary. As you work with your dreams you will begin to find meanings that aren't described here, and to interpret many dream symbols for which Cayce never offered an interpretation. In the back of your dream journal you can compile a supplemental list of entries for quick reference.

Ambulance

1. Help for the physical body that can be brought into play.

> Dreamer (male, age 26) sees a horse that is hitched to an ambulance. It is rushing toward him.

OTHER POSSIBILITIES: 2. Impending emergency.

Anchor

1. Staying in one spot in understanding (i.e., "taking up anchor" means starting to learn).

> Dreamer (male, age 30) watches a woman get on a ferryboat. She lifts the anchor and starts the boat by herself. The dreamer says, "If I had known she was going to get on that boat all alone, I would have helped her."

OTHER POSSIBILITIES: 2. Tied down. 3. Stability. 4. Power of determination and resolve from deep within. 5. Desire to settle down.

Angel

1. The light of truth.

> Dreamer (female, age 46) is suspended above the deck of a boat in a hammock, which rocks to and fro dangerously over the side of the boat. She worries what would happen to her if she fell off into the ocean. She affirms that God's will be done, and then sees in the sky a beautiful, white-robed angel.

OTHER POSSIBILITIES: 2. Wisdom. 3. Guidance. 4. A coming birth or death (literally or figuratively).

Armor

1. "The armor of the Lord" that can protect a person from difficulties and temptations.

> Dreamer (male, age 58) in this vision sees a chariot in the air, with four white horses and a man driving. The same man suddenly appears nearby, dressed in armor, with a shield and a cape but no weapons. He raises his hand in salute to the dreamer and says, "The chariot of the Lord and the horseman thereof."

OTHER POSSIBILITIES: 2. Rigidity. 3. Barriers we put up to people in self-defense.

Arrow

1. A coming message—full of power, intent, and purpose.

> Dreamer (male, age 27) sees an arrow shot from a bow. It travels high and with great power.

OTHER POSSIBILITIES: **2.** Smitten by love (i.e., Cupid's arrow). **3.** Vengeance.

Baby

1. A new venture.

> Dreamer (female, age 47) sees Edgar Cayce and herself in a room with a baby. Something is wrong with the baby, so Cayce undresses the baby and puts it in a bowl of hot water. When he begins to add more hot water, the dreamer sees it may burn the baby. She intervenes and shows Cayce how to do it better.

2. A new interpersonal relationship.

> Dreamer (male, age 28) is with a business associate whose wife has recently given birth. The child is beautiful but also has defective feet.

3. That which appears to be small or of little account but may be of the greatest value.

> Dreamer (male, age 56) sees a remarkable baby who is talking before an audience. Everyone is amazed, though skeptical at first that it might be only a midget disguised as a baby. But a careful examination shows that it is a baby—a prodigy.

4. A spiritual truth.

> Same dream as immediately above—the Cayce reading offered two levels of interpretation for the same symbol in this dream.

5. That which requires teaching, guidance, and direction.

> Dreamer (male, age 30) is standing in a rowboat and his wife is pulling him in to shore. Some people begin to carry her and she seems to turn into a baby.

6. The harmonious union of two people.

> Dreamer (male, age 30) sees that his wife gave birth to triplets. [Additional note from Cayce's interpretation: the three babies represent harmonious relations between the dreamer and his wife at physical, mental, and spiritual levels.]

7. Becoming open and unfearful in the sense that Jesus spoke: "except you become as little chidren . . ."

> Dreamer (male, age 33) sees a baby who shows no signs of fear.

OTHER POSSIBILITIES: **8.** Undeveloped, immature. **9.** Something just getting started. **10.** Free of responsibilities. **11.** Something needing nurturance and encouragement.

Ball

1. The "perfect sphere": some ideal or concept of wholeness.

> Dreamer (male, age 30) is playing baseball with his brother and his mother.

2. The forces of this world as they relate to the Universal Force.

> Dreamer (male, age 30) is playing croquet with his Father and has only three more wickets to hit the ball through. "Almost through," he says, but then realizes they are the three hardest wickets to make.

3. A whole, or well-rounded, approach to things.

> Dreamer (male, age 30) is watching the Penn-Yale college football game. He has ambivalent currents of sentiment about who he wants to win. He sees Yale score a touchdown by an elaborate passing of the ball from one player to another to another.

4. The oneness of purpose.

> Dreamer (male, age 30) sees a billiard table and many balls rolling on it. Then he sees many other items pertaining to his new home.

5. Childhood games.

> Dreamer (male, age 27) sees a ball that belongs to his wife. It has a vicious little animal in it. He hits it with a broom and knocks it into their bed and under the covers. His wife begins to cry because this ball/ animal is in the bed and the dreamer takes her out because of his fear for her safety. [Note: Cayce's interpretation is that the man should avoid vicious, childish game-playing with his wife. Keep things out in the open, not hidden (i.e., not "covered up").]

OTHER POSSIBILITIES: **6.** Completeness. **7.** Competitiveness.

Bath

1. Cleansing and freeing from old ideas.

> Dreamer (male, age 30) is taking a shower in an odd sort of place, and the bottom of the tub is all black. The dirty surroundings don't appeal to him.

2. A cleansing and strengthening of the outer self, which should not be confused with the inner strengthening that comes from God.

> Dreamer (male, 30) is not feeling well physically, and a nurse is in attendance. He is warned that he should not bathe, but he does anyway. Upon coming out he says he is very weak, falls into the nurse's arms, and reaches for his heart.

OTHER POSSIBILITIES: 3. Physical cleansing. 4. Letting go of opinions and prejudices. 5. Baptism.

Bear

1. That which has two sides: one destructive and the other playful, caressing, and loving.

> Dreamer (male, age 49) is in an enclosure with many animals and birds. He hears a commotion behind him that he knows is a warning to him that he is in danger. He sees behind him a bear sitting on its haunches, with its arms outstretched. He awakens in fright, wondering if the bear meant to harm him or hug him lovingly.

OTHER POSSIBILITIES: 2. Grumpy. 3. Overprotectiveness. 4. Falling stock prices ("bear market"). 5. Hibernating; retreating.

Bed

1. Sexual activity.

> Dreamer (female, age 20) sees a woman stretched out on a bed with the bedsprings swaying back and forth. Something inside the dreamer says, "You will awaken to something different," and she feels a smile on her face.

2. Dirty conditions in the bed—care must be taken that by moral standards one's life appears to be clean and open.

> Dreamer (male, age 48) sees someone climb into bed with him. Dreamer is putting on funny-looking shoes with peculiar shoestrings.

3. Closeness to another; intimacy.

> Dreamer (male, age 30) sees many shining lights, each of which he knows is a discarnate spirit-being. He senses that one is his deceased father. The dreamer's wife suggests that he turn out the electric light in the room; and, upon doing so, his father appears in bed with him. The dreamer cries from the intense emotion of this reunion, and they

exchange affirmations of love for each other. [Note: Cayce's interpretation is that the father in bed with the dreamer is an actual soul-to-soul contact.]

OTHER POSSIBILITIES: **4.** Rest or sleep. **5.** Unconsciousness.

Bird

1. The bearer of a message.

[Note: Cayce clairvoyantly interpreted this dream before it was read, so no record exists of what the exact dream was.]

2. Canaries: idle talk (like chirping and twittering) that is a hindrance to oneself.

Dreamer (female, age unknown) sees some canaries and is working to help heal them.

3. Eagle: the highest elements of power and might in action.

Dreamer (male, age 30) sees a metal eagle flying over the ocean. The metallic bird soars high and low, sometimes wavering and almost dropping in the water. Finally it lands safely on the earth.

OTHER POSSIBILITIES: **4.** Freedom from material ties. **5.** The soul. **6.** Spiritual knowledge. **7.** The heart chakra. **8.** Aspirations, thoughts, and ideals. **9.** Telepathy. **10.** The higher self.

Black

1. Obstructions.

Dreamer (male, age 30) wonders why he hasn't been having visions lately. Immediately he sees himself in a store selecting from among many veils. Most of the veils are black. He picks six to cover his face.

OTHER POSSIBILITIES: **2.** The unconscious mind. **3.** A rejected aspect of oneself. **4.** That which exists as potential but is not developed yet. **5.** Temptation or evil. **6.** Mystery.

Black man

1. A truth that is submerged and still in one's own unconscious (for a non-black dreamer).

Dreamer (white female, age 48) sees a black man who is being led to the gallows, where a great crowd of people have gathered. Just as they are about to slip the noose over his head, he gets away, crawling desperately and speedily through the crowd.

Blanket, Quilt, Bed Cover

1. The "cover" or mode of conduct in the home.

    Dreamer (male, age 30) sees many accessories and items pertaining to his new home. He especially notes the quilts. A voice speaks to him about jealousy and envy.

2. Making the best of something; trying to cover a difficult situation.

    Dreamer (male, age 30) is in a room with his mother-in-law. She is sick in bed with a red-spotted gray wool blanket over her. She says that she provided the material for it—why didn't he make a prettier and better one out of it? Dreamer responds that he didn't have time because he wanted to do his writing.

3. Covered or hidden.

    Dreamer (male, age 27) sees a ball that belongs to his wife. It has a vicious little animal in it. He hits it with a broom and knocks it into their bed and under the covers. His wife begins to cry because this ball/animal is in the bed and the dreamer takes her out because of his fear for her safety. [Note: Cayce's interpretation is to avoid vicious, childish game-playing with his wife. Keep things out in the open, not hidden (i.e., not "covered up").]

Blood

1. The physical forces of the body itself, indicative of the relative level of health or imbalance.

    Dreamer (male, age 31) is spitting up blood into his handkerchief. He is frightened that the bleeding is indicative of tuberculosis.

2. The ideas and ideals of a person (e.g., a blood transfusion representing their transmission).

    Dreamer (male, age 31) receives a transfusion of his wife's blood in order to enrich his blood supply and to get needed strength.

3. Life-giving, vital force.

    This interpretation of blood as an archetype was volunteered in one Cayce reading (female, age 25).

4. Strength (i.e., as in the strength that comes to us through the blood shed by Christ).

> Dreamer (male, age 31) sees his deceased father appear as a counselor and guardian. But the father is tired and has drops of blood on his neck.

OTHER POSSIBILITIES: **5.** The sacrifice of Christ. **6.** Kinship (i.e., as in "blood ties"). **7.** Animosity (i.e., as in the phrase "bad blood").

Blue

1. Truth

> Dreamer (female, age 21) is back at her college, watching a basketball game in the school gymnasium. She sees that she and all her sorority sisters are dressed alike, with white dresses and blue ties.

OTHER POSSIBILITIES: **2.** Religious or spiritual feelings. **3.** Calm, contemplative, peaceful. **4.** Will, personal or divine. **5.** Healing. [See also GYMNASIUM.]

Boat

1. The voyage of life.

> Dreamer (female, age 21) is on a boat where there is much thundering and fighting. The boat is struck by lightning and the boiler explodes. The boat sinks and they are killed.

2. A body of thought that one can enter into and travel upon.

> Dreamer (male, age 30) and a male companion are sitting by the beach watching an old, wrecked ship drift toward the shore. It continually rises and sinks in the waves as water fills up and then rushes out of the holes in its sides. It finally comes to rest on the beach.

3. Something that comes from a foreign source (i.e., from across the waters).

> Dreamer (male, age 30) is sitting in his former home with his parents and brother. They are discussing the cost of a boat trip to Europe.

4. A forthcoming trip.

> Dreamer (female, age 22) sees a huge boat with her brother-in-law and sister-in-law aboard. He is very sick and dies. Her sister-in-law appears in a mourning veil. [Note: Cayce's interpretation warns that the dreamer might become seasick on a planned boat trip.]

5. A message about spiritual truth to be carried abroad.

> Dreamer (male, age 31) is captain of a great ocean liner. At a dinner on board he makes an announcement: Last night there was a terrible storm in which he lost control of the ship. He had prayed and God had delivered them safely. However, the people at the dinner seem unconcerned and don't realize how important this was.

6. The soul or after-death body.

> Dreamer (male, age 32) sees a ferryboat separating from the pier as it begins a journey. [Note: Cayce's interpretation was that this vision symbolized the way in which the soul departs the physical world at death. However, it was *not* predictive of impending death for the dreamer.]

OTHER POSSIBILITIES: 7. Having common problems or challenges, as those of other people depicted in the boat (i.e., "in the same boat"). 8. An adventure. 9. Beginning to explore the unconscious mind. 10. An opportunity (e.g., "missing the boat").

Book

1. Knowledge.

> Dreamer (male, age 30) visits the parents of a former college friend. He gives them a simplified edition of a book about an automotive company. They hand him a more complicated, lengthy edition, which he starts to read.

2. Lessons gained.

> Dreamer (male, age 30) is back in college again. In the evening goes to the bookstore to buy a volume about world history. He is disappointed to hear that he is too late—the store has closed for the day.

OTHER POSSIBILITIES: 3. Memories. 4. Ideas. 5. Akashic records (universal knowledge of all historic events and human experiences).

Box

1. That which holds and protects.

> Dreamer (male, age 41) experiences himself separating his physical self from his soul self. His physical self is encased in a box.

2. The conditions surrounding a person's life.

> Dreamer (male, age 30) sees claylike boxes and humanlike figures inside them.

3. Hedged in or boxed in.

> Dreamer (male, age 30) is in a darkened room where he sees a box with a light inside it. The light is revolving on a tripod, throwing its beams all about.

4. Being hemmed in by the cares of the world.

> Dreamer (male, age 30) sees a box and people gathered around it, weeping.

Bread

1. The most basic sustaining force of life; the staff of life; that which permits development ("morally, mentally, spiritually, financially").

> Dreamer (female, age 21) walks through a woods with her husband and other family members. They are to prepare dinner when they arrive at their destination. One person in the group finds a long cabinet and opens it. There is a skeleton inside and most of them run in fear; but when they look back they see that it's really a loaf of bread.

2. Positive efforts invested in the present that may have future benefits (i.e, biblical metaphor: casting bread upon the waters, and "it shall be returned to thee").

> Dreamer (male, age 31) sees a woman with her baby granddaughter. The woman asks for and receives from dreamer forgiveness for past misdeeds. Then dreamer offers pieces of two bread rolls to the baby and speaks lovingly to it.

OTHER POSSIBILITIES: 3. That which has been learned from life. 4. Money.

Bricks

1. Little words or little deeds that can slowly be built up.

> Dreamer (male, age 32) gets into great trouble over his efforts to push down the brick front of a business associate's home. The dreamer offers to have a bricklayer come and repair the damage tomorrow, but the dreamer must try to temporarily fix things immediately—patching up the damage by putting in bricks one at a time.

OTHER POSSIBILITIES: 2. Hardness. 3. Strength.

Bridge

1. Our way of passing through material life.

    Dreamer (male, age 30) sees two ways to cross river: an upper bridge and a lower one. Other people are using the lower bridge, so the dreamer does too. However, it seems dangerous to him.

2. The foundation for a way of life.

    Dreamer (male, age 30) sees a huge new concrete bridge and is especially taken by its wonderful $10 million foundation.

3. A transition.

    Dreamer (female, age 21) sees a body of water and a bridge crossing it. She and a few others are crossing it, then they see a church and hear singing.

    OTHER POSSIBILITIES: 4. A link between opposites. 5. A way of overcoming a difficulty.

Bull

1. Hardheadedness or stubbornness (i.e., "bullheaded").

    Dreamer (male, age 48) sees a bull with a funny-looking head.

2. Bull market.

    Dreamer (male, age 30), who is a stockbroker in waking life, sees a bull following his wife's red dress. He tries to catch the bull.

    OTHER POSSIBILITIES: 3. Sexuality or sexual appetite. 4. The first chakra or spiritual center.

Bull's-Eye

1. Attunement to one's ideals or goal.

    Dreamer (male, age 30) is target shooting with a gun. He's trying hard to get his sight on the center of the bull's-eye, and by his third shot he is beginning to hit close to it.

    OTHER POSSIBILITIES: 2. A state of feeling centered. 3. The target of attack by others. 4. A point of success or accomplishment.

Burglar

1. A warning about someone who may try to take advantage of the dreamer.

    Dreamer (male, age 44) is in his apartment with his business partner. They are crawling on the floor trying to get away from burglars.

OTHER POSSIBILITIES: **2.** Negative attitude or emotion that is stealing one's energy or vitality. **3.** Guilt about having taken something (literally or metaphorically) from someone. **4.** Desire to take something from someone (e.g., power, prestige, etc.). **5.** Fear of being robbed.

Cake

1. Aggrandizement of physical appetites.

> Dreamer (male, age 30) sees a cake, like a birthday cake, with lighted candles.

OTHER POSSIBILITIES: **2.** Something luxurious or not practical. **3.** Reward. **4.** Celebration.

Candle

1. Singleness of purpose and heart.

> Dreamer (male, age 32) is in a room with many relatives and the question comes up about the amount of money left to his wife by his father. He gives a premeditated answer—$80,000—but it meets with skeptical looks. Dreamer then sees the face of his father looking at him strangely, and he notes the sight of burning candle lights.

2. Stages of development.

> Dreamer (male, age 31) sees a man carefully counting five candles. He doesn't grasp the meaning of it and the man says, "Now pay attention—watch closely," and he counts them again.

OTHER POSSIBILITIES: **3.** Personal physical resources (e.g., "burning a candle at both ends"). **4.** Enlightenment; wisdom.

Candy

1. One's own physical satisfaction; self-indulgence.

> Dreamer (female, age 21) has $6 and plans to buy her husband some ties. But she finds they are too expensive and goes to a candy store instead. She orders a bag of jelly beans, then changes her order to an even larger bag.

2. Improper, indulgent eating.

> Dreamer (female, age 22) and her husband watch many children being killed in car accidents. Then they move on and go to a candy store.

Her husband buys candy and she chastises him, "You know it's not good for you and you should not eat it."

3. A luxury.

Dreamer (male, age 31) is in a railroad station and buys many boxes of candy for a dollar each, anticipating that he can sell them for twice as much.

4. Sweets: diet reference to amount of sweets.

Dreamer (female, age 21) is sitting at a table eating large quantities of sweets. She is packing it in and having a great time.

Cane

1. That which provides aid or assistance (especially in a physical way) *but* which can be used either as mere "show" *or* as genuine help (i.e., some people carry a cane only for show, others really need it to walk).

Dreamer (male, age 27) is at a social gathering and when he starts to leave cannot find his silver-topped cane. He looks everywhere, but then remembers that he didn't bring it with him.

OTHER POSSIBILITIES: **2.** Support. **3.** Discipline. **4.** Male sex organ.

Captain

1. The one in charge (e.g., boat captain) and *accountable* for the lives and well-being of others.

Dreamer (male, age 31) is aboard an ocean liner with many passengers. He is the captain, and at a dinner party he rises to make an announcement, but the passengers seem to ignore him.

OTHER POSSIBILITIES: **2.** Higher self. **3.** Intellect. **4.** Source of guidance. **5.** Authority, power.

Car/Automobile

1. The vehicle or means by which we move through the journey of life.

Dreamer (male, age 62) is driving a car with his wife as passenger. They drive through a narrow passage, over a muddy place where many other cars have gotten stuck, and finally come to a good road.

2. Automobile stock.

Dreamer (male, age 31), who is a stockbroker in waking life, sees himself in an auto garage. He is trying to get his auto out of the crowded garage.

3. Car accident: general warning about upcoming period of being accident-prone—not necessarily a literal car accident.

> Dreamer (female, age 21) sees herself in an auto accident in which she receives a concussion.

4. Speeding car: hurrying or forcing an issue.

> Dreamer (male, age 30) is in a hurry and so he speeds in his automobile. But the police catch him and pull him over, thus slowing him down in his trip even more than if he had not been speeding.

OTHER POSSIBILITIES: **5.** Physical body. **6.** Etheric body. **7.** One's ideas or mind-set. **8.** Ambitious and driven. **9.** Status or social standing. **10.** Self-control or lack of it (who is driving?).

Carpet

1. A subservient state; being walked on.

> Dreamer (male, age 48) remembers only a dream fragment in which he saw a carpet, a bull, and a hammer.

OTHER POSSIBILITIES: **2.** Insulation against worldly influences. **3.** Softness, comfort. **4.** The handiwork of God. **5.** Hiding or covering up something.

Cat

1. Sexuality.

> Dreamer (male, age 31) is bitten on the arm by a cat and he orders the cat away. Then he sees two "married" birds who are mating and are bothered by a third bird, which they throw off.

2. Kitten: prankster.

> Dreamer (male, age 31) is with his mother. They are looking for a kitten, which keeps eluding them.

OTHER POSSIBILITIES: **3.** Independent. **4.** Gossipy.

Chewing Gum

1. That which must be chewed upon, as a message or lesson, in order to be understood.

> Dreamer (male, age 30) has a visionary experience in which his deceased father appears to him. The father opens a box revealing four

pieces of chewing gum, and he invites the dreamer to chew on a couple of them.

OTHER POSSIBILITIES: 2. Repetitive, habitual patterns of eating or of speech. 3. Childishness. 4. Lacking substance or nourishment—i.e., chewing gum is taken into the mouth like food, but is never swallowed and digested.

Children

1. Hope.

Dreamer (female, age 55) explores the area around a large waterfront home. There is a lake with clear water and swans being fed by happy children.

2. Simplicity.

Dreamer (male, age 32) fights with a great giant and things are going badly. Suddenly, a small child appears to make a pronouncement and that stops the giant. [Note: Cayce's interpretation was that the giant represents ridicule heaped on the dreamer for having espoused complex spiritual truth—ridicule that makes him feel small. The child shows the solutions: present truth in its simplicity.]

3. That which is undeveloped (i.e., "when I was a child, I thought as a child, but now . . .").

Dreamer (female, age 29) sees a boy child whom she recognizes to be weak-minded.

4. Responsibilities (i.e., adult parents are required to assume responsibility for the well-being of their children).

Dreamer (male, age 30) comes into a room where he sees two small children and his brother. Dreamer supervises their play.

5. Those who will ask and seek to learn.

Dreamer (male, age 30, Jewish) is teaching to the many sects of the Jewish faith. A Christian lady enters with her child, although many of the gathered people try to refuse her. She wants her boy to learn what the dreamer is teaching.

OTHER POSSIBILITIES: 6. Childishness. 7. Some personal endeavor that is about the same age as the children.

Church

1. Safety, security, and strength in the spiritual forces.

   Dreamer (male, age 43) tries to escape with his family the rising waters of a tidal wave. They go up a hill and find a church. With the water at their heels they start to scale the walls of the church.

2. Conditions related to both daily life *and* spiritual life.

   Dreamer (male, age 18) is in a church where a collection is being taken. Everyone is giving liberally. Then the church members begin to discuss critically a woman the dreamer knows. He takes up for her, arguing her case.

OTHER POSSIBILITIES: 3. One's religious beliefs. 4. Childhood associations with religion. 5. One's entire being (physical, mental, and spiritual).

Cliff

1. A place of heightened knowledge or understanding.

   Dreamer (male, age 30) sees his wife swimming across a large body of water. It is dangerous, but her goal is to reach a man standing on the cliff at the opposite shore. She makes it across and hands a silver cup (like a trophy cup) to the man, who has now become the dreamer himself.

OTHER POSSIBILITIES: 2. High ideals. 3. An obstacle to surmount. 4. Ambition.

Clothing

1. The physical, material body (i.e., the soul "clothes" itself in a material body).

   Dreamer (male, age 29) is with his mother and she recognizes a spot on the suit of clothes he is wearing.

2. The outer personality patterns (i.e., attitudes and behavior).

   Dreamer (male, age 55) sees a friend come to breakfast. She is fussing because everyone is bothering her. Dreamer reaches over to fight with her; but as he touches her, he notices her new suit coat: reddish, brown-checked, and very shiny.

OTHER POSSIBILITIES: 3. Your occupation, the vocational role you wear.
4. Reference to a part of the physical body that the piece of clothing covers.
5. The persona or face we show to the world.

Clover

1. That which grows and develops in a well-rounded way.

   Dreamer (male, 30) sits at the bottom of a hill with a friend. They see many little clovers that line the ridges of the hill.

2. Four-leaf clover: seeming "good luck" that really has a spiritual cause.

   Dreamer (female, age 21) notices that her husband has a four-leaf clover in a soap dish. After some occurrence they disagree whether or not it brought good or bad luck.

Coat

1. Thoughts and attitudes.

   Dreamer (male, age 27) is wearing his brown suit coat and it gets dirty: a big ink stain on the lapel. He feels the suit is ruined.

2. Attitudes (with color of coat giving clue as to type of attitude).

   Dreamer (male, age 55) sees a friend come to breakfast. She is fussing because everyone is bothering her. Dreamer reaches over to fight with her; but as he touches her, he notices her new suit coat: reddish, brown-checked, and very shiny.

3. Raincoat: recommendation regarding physical health—to stay dry in order to avoid a virus cold.

   Dreamer (male, age 27) is riding on a trolley car in his old hometown. He loses his raincoat and the trolley runs over it.

4. Fur coat: wintertime.

   Dreamer (male, age 30, who is a stockbroker in waking life) is in his office and finds that he has 500 shares of Reading Railroad stock in his pocket. He leaves the office with his fur overcoat. [Note: Cayce's interpretation was a precognitive dream indicating a change in the monetary value of Reading Railroad stock in the coming wintertime.]

   OTHER POSSIBILITIES: 5. Raincoat—protection from one's own emotional upset or that of others.

Coffin

1. The nature of the death experience.

   Dreamer (male, age 30) sees himself and another person in a coffin, buried in a grave. Both are alive. Dreamer speculates about what he will find to be the nature of the afterlife.

2. A state of consciousness that is attuned to the unseen spiritual world.

   Dreamer (male, age 31) reaches inside his father's coffin but withdraws his hand at the thought of decayed flesh. He says to his brother that they should be able to see spirits of the deceased. Nearby they see a shadowy image they know to be their uncle.

3. A weakened state; total lack of vitality.

   Dreamer (male, age 48) is in a beautiful, large home—and yet it has a dismal, dark entrance. A friend comes to the door to announce that his son has died at college and asks if the coffin could temporarily be placed here in the dreamer's home. Soon the body arrives in its casket.

4. A deadened, dull, unawakened state of consciousness lacking in spiritual insight.

   Same dream as 3, above. The Cayce reading offered two levels of interpretation for the same symbol in this dream.

   OTHER POSSIBILITIES: See all references under DEATH.

Colors

See references under BLACK, BLUE, GOLDEN, GREEN, RED, WHITE.

Compass

1. A source of guidance.

   Dreamer (male, age 49) sees himself with his grandparents and he has a compass.

   OTHER POSSIBILITIES: 2. The most fulfilling direction in life. 3. The ability to persist in the face of opposing outer events.

Container

1. Saucer: all that is currently held in the conscious mind.

   Dreamer (male, age 30) twice sees a china saucer break or a piece chip off.

2. Received like a trophy cup: the attainment of a union of knowledge and understanding, which brings happiness, joy, and peace.

   Dreamer (male, age 30) sees his wife swimming across a large body of water. It is dangerous, but her goal is to reach a man standing on the cliff at the opposite shore. She makes it across and hands a silver cup (like a trophy cup) to the man, who has now become the dreamer himself.

OTHER POSSIBILITIES: **3.** Receptivity. **4.** Female sex organs. **5.** All one's inner contents—the soul.

Court-Martial/Court Trial

1. Criticism (from others or self).

Dreamer (male, age 44) climbs a fence to explore a fountain area and is arrested by military guards. He is taken to a court-martial before a tribunal. He is found guilty.

OTHER POSSIBILITIES: **2.** Measuring one's own recent behavior against universal laws. **3.** A difficult or "trying" experience.

Dawn (Morning)

1. The awakening of new forces.

Dreamer (male, age 29) asked for a dream interpretation reading, but no dream was given. Cayce interpreted the dream clairvoyantly without it being read to him.

OTHER POSSIBILITIES: **2.** A healing. **3.** A fresh perspective or new approach. **4.** A breakthrough in understanding.

Death (Dying)

1. Birth of new thought, an awakening from the subconscious mind.

Dreamer (female, age 20) dreams simply that she has died.

2. The coming of a condition that will *test* one's abilities.

Dreamer (male, age 48) is in a beautiful, large home—and yet it has a dismal, dark entrance. A friend comes to the door to announce that his son has died at college and asks if the coffin could temporarily be placed here in the dreamer's home. Soon the body arrives in its casket.

3. Trials and tribulations that provide lessons in spiritual truth.

Dreamer (male, age 30) sees his wife weeping over the death of her mother. [Note: Cayce's interpretation was specifically that in this case "death" was symbolic and there was no need to fear an impending death of the dreamer's mother-in-law.]

4. Death of dreamer's brother: the death of the Christ, the Elder Brother, and its significance to the world.

Dreamer (male, age 30) dreams that his brother has died of a stroke. He is overcome with grief, but then realizes that this tragedy coincides with his own calling to teach to masses of people the ideas advanced by the Christ.

5. Loss of a talent because of defects, imbalances, or weaknesses in the physical body.

Dreamer (male, age 49) experiences himself scalding to death in a bathtub.

6. The equalizer (i.e., that which brings all people of different social standing to one level).

Dreamer (female, age 23) and her mother watch an acquaintance who is lying out in a public place dying. They watch the final stages and see him die. Dreamer starts to cry but her mother instructs her not to.

7. One's own after-death state: the consciousness and understanding you experience in the after-death is *available* to you *now* as a way of understanding and comprehending in the physical plane.

Dreamer (female, age 23) is sitting in a room with her mother and husband, but she knows that she herself is dead. She wonders if they can see her. The dreamer's aunt comes in, and from her behavior the dreamer realizes that she is invisible to them.

8. The loss of a *characteristic* from one's own life that is also a characteristic of the person who has died in the dream.

Dreamer (male, age 30) is at a board meeting of prominent men—scholars, philosophers, great minds. He is to address the group, but breaks down crying when he realizes his brother isn't there and is dead.

9. The need for more attention, sympathy, and love *for* the one who dies in the dream.

Dreamer (male, age 31) has a fight with his wife in which he beats her into unconsciousness. Too late he becomes remorseful and she lies dying in his arms as the dream ends.

10. Transition or change.

Dreamer (male, age 32) sees a woman with two children, one dead and the other dying. He tries, using mind power, to bring the soul of the dead child back. Then he and the dreamer climb steps.

Diamond

1. Great truth.

Dreamer (male, age 31) has been given several pieces of diamond jewelry as security for shares of stock he has purchased. He shows the diamonds to family members and others, who want to see what security this company offers to those who buy its stock.

OTHER POSSIBILITIES: **2.** The eternity of the spirit. **3.** Spiritual consciousness. **4.** Hardness. **5.** Something of great value. **6.** Money; financial security. **7.** Love or being loved.

Dining Table

1. Attention to physical food; diet.

Dreamer (male, age 31) is seated at a large dinner table with many others. A steak dinner is served. Then there is a second dinner affair at the same table with a similar bill of fare. Dreamer complains about certain arrangements not having been followed properly.

2. What one is feeding the mind.

Dreamer (male, age 30) sees his dining room furniture and hears a voice that speaks about causes and their effects.

Dirt/Dirty

1. Something unbecoming or improper in oneself that needs to be corrected.

Dreamer (male, age 31) is looking at himself in the mirror. He is wearing a new blue-striped shirt. Although he thinks it is pretty, an unseen voice calls his attention to how it is soiled.

2. Fear or "dirty attitudes" within oneself.

Dreamer (male, age 45) is working on his car. His shirt gets dirty and he goes to change it. While he is gone, someone takes his car.

3. Improper or unclean state of mind.

Dreamer (male, age 27) is wearing his brown suit coat and it gets a big, dirty ink stain on the lapel when his fountain pen leaks. He feels the suit is ruined.

4. Warning to keep life "clean" and avoid any appearance of questionable moral conduct.

Dreamer (male, age 48) is in a room with dirty conditions all about. Someone gets in bed with him.

5. Too much grease in diet, which can be harmful.

> Dreamer (male, age 55) sees that he has gotten grease on his trousers and wonders if the soiled spot will come clean. But when he comes outside into the light it seems to disappear.

Diving

1. Jumping into a new life experience, perhaps not as carefully as it should be done.

> Dreamer (female, age 21) stands on a rickety old platform beside a body of water. She tries to dive in, but does a painful belly-whopper.

OTHER POSSIBILITIES: 2. Enthusiasm. 3. Going into something with your head (i.e., intellect) leading the way.

Dog

1. A nature or disposition that may not always be trusted.

> Dreamer (male, age 49) has an enclosure (a high wire fence) with animals inside: a bear, goat, deer, geese, fox, wolf, and dog. The dog is one he knows in waking life.

2. That which is faithful *and* unfaithful.

> Dreamer (female, age 21) sees a dog and a strange fire.

3. That which is friendly or, if aroused, an enemy.

> Dreamer (male, age 50) is with his wife and secretary looking for his deceased grandmother, whom he has heard is alive again. They find her in a basement with vines growing around her. As they start to leave they encounter three dogs, one of whom gets loose and runs toward the grandmother's body.

4. Things going downhill, going "to the dogs."

> Same dream as for 3, above. Cayce gave two interpretations of the same symbol for this dream.

OTHER POSSIBILITIES: 5. Aggressiveness. 6. Instinctive knowledge. 7. Obedience.

Donkey

1. An honor.

> Dreamer (female, age 59) sees a strange man and then sees herself riding on donkeys. [Note: Cayce's interpretation of the strange man

was the Christ himself. The donkey ride was reminiscent of the great honor given to him on Palm Sunday.]

2. A lowly position, indicating either dishonor or humbleness.

Same dream as for 1, above. Cayce gave a second interpretation for the same symbol. That is, a donkey also meant "dishonor," because to her conscious attitudes the donkey is such a lowly animal. Cayce's final interpretative comment addressed this paradox: Act in a humble way that doesn't draw attention to yourself; be in authority but don't give orders.

OTHER POSSIBILITIES: 3. Stubborn and unyielding. 4. Bearer of a heavy load.

Door/Doorway

1. Openings, ways, or avenues of personal expression.

Dreamer (male, age 29) sees a door slamming and hears the order to "Get out!"

2. Locking back door: wanting to avoid unpleasant conditions.

Dreamer (male, age 48) is preparing to leave his home. He is locking the back door when his son calls him. They look out the front door to see many friends and family members arriving with their suitcases.

3. Front door: the place of meeting that which is newly coming into one's life.

Same dream as for 2, above. Cayce's interpretation of friends and family: those people who would be coming for help in the future.

4. Trap door—a coming and unexpected new disclosure.

Dreamer (male, age 31) sees a trap door and a man who seems ready to open it.

5. Trap door: traps or pitfalls into which one can fall.

Dreamer (male, age 55) is trying to get somewhere with his family, but they turn to go another direction. He follows someone's advice to enter through a doorway. But as he does it turns into a trap door, and he finds himself in a basement from which he can't escape.

6. Closing doors—counted-on opportunities will be shut, causing consternation.

Dreamer (male, age 31) gets off a train at the station and notices that he cannot get aboard again because the doors of the cars are closing. He is dismayed and looks for help.

OTHER POSSIBILITIES: **7.** A barrier that potentially can be removed. **8.** Death.

Dragon

1. Fear.

> Dreamer (male, age 31) sees a girl whom he knows to represent wisdom and inner power. She throws a stone into space—it passes like a shooting star, then hits two caged dragons and draws them down to earth. They move about the earth. They do no harm, but the dreamer greatly fears them.

OTHER POSSIBILITIES: **2.** Materialism. **3.** Repressed emotion. **4.** The power of the unconscious.

Drama

1. The acts of the play are phases in the dreamer's own life being symbolically replayed.

> Dreamer (male, age 31) goes to a theater with his wife. They watch a three-act play, each part of which has its own elaborate story line.

Draperies

1. That which covers or hides.

> Dreamer (male, age 30) sees a bookcase with a glass door of which the glass is cracked. A voice says, "We have drapes to cover that here."

OTHER POSSIBILITIES: **2.** Adornment. **3.** Privacy or the desire for it.

Dress

1. (New) one being tried on—new thought, new ideals.

> Dreamer (female, age 21) is shopping for a new dress with her mother. Dreamer has her hair arranged like a turban. She tries on a dress, which the saleswoman says is pretty; but her mother and another saleswoman disagree.

2. One's appearance in the eyes of others.

> Dreamer (female, age 21) is at her summer home with her mother and others. She has on a gingham dress. Her mother and a friend disagree about how she looks in that dress.

3. The identity or the self-image one has adopted or is "wearing."

> Dreamer (female, age 21) sees herself in a blue-and-white dress, kneeling before her mother's doctor. She says to him, "Through you and God our mother has been spared." [Note: Cayce interpreted the blue-and-white dress to show her own pure, true identity coming through.]

Drugstore

1. Actual drugs taken by the body.

> Dreamer (male, age 32) and his brother are going to visit relatives but plan to stop at a certain drugstore on the way. It turns out to be in a tough, dangerous area with many threatening people lurking about. Dreamer is frightened.

OTHER POSSIBILITIES: 2. Healing. 3. Reliance on physical means to stimulate change.

Drum

1. Beating: undiplomatic or untactful, "beating the drum" of one's own point of view.

> Dreamer (male, age 32) sees a beating drum. He has the feeling it has something to do with a company with which he has business dealings.

OTHER POSSIBILITIES: 2. Heart; pulse. 3. Rhythms in one's life.

Duel

1. Sword: verbal fight with another person.

> Dreamer (male, age 32) is having a sword duel with his wife. She strikes him on the head, splitting it open. A voice says, "Remember last October." [Note: Dream occurred in April following verbal fight with wife in October.]

OTHER POSSIBILITIES: 2. Internal fight between two sides of oneself. 3. Self-criticism or self-condemnation.

Dummy

1. Warning about getting involved with dim-witted individuals.

> Dreamer (male, age 28) sees a dummy. It is wearing a woman's blue suit, has no head, and is sitting on his bed.

2. That which is controlled or yanked around by outside forces.

Dreamer (male, age 31) sees a dummy (puppet) on the stage of the theater. A man behind the stage curtain tells him to pull the string. When he does it brings forth many acrobats.

OTHER POSSIBILITIES: **3.** One's own stupidity. **4.** A false, artificial side of oneself.

Dynamite

1. Temper.

Dreamer (male, age 30) receives a verbal warning not to break dynamite.

OTHER POSSIBILITIES: **2.** Material force. **3.** Explosive emotions (including fears).

Electric Power Line

1. The driving force that energizes a situation.

Dreamer (male, age 30) is with a business friend riding on a trolley car. They watch how the conductor of another trolley can control the trolley pole, which connects to an overhead electrical wire.

Elephant

1. Power and might combined with heightened knowledge and cunning.

Dreamer (male, age 15) is picked up by an elephant. The elephant has a keeper who is of assistance.

2. Knowledge and power.

Dreamer (male, age 30) sees three elephants, each of which is shooting cannonballs out of its mouth toward a target.

OTHER POSSIBILITIES: **3.** Sexuality. **4.** The great inner power of the unconscious. **5.** Strength of will. **6.** Long memory; unforgetting. **7.** Thick skinned.

Elevator

1. Changes; ups and downs.

Dreamer (male, age 30) gets on an elevator. It seems to make a stop at each floor.

OTHER POSSIBILITIES: **2.** Altered states of consciousness.

Explosion

1. Warning of turmoil or change.

> Dreamer (female, age 21) is on a boat trip with her husband. There is considerable shooting and fighting on board. Finally, the boat is struck by lightning and the whole boat explodes. It sinks and they are killed.

2. Harsh responses likely to come from others due to recent behavior of dreamer.

> Dreamer (female, age 22) is out walking and passes a contraption that is going to cause an explosion. She runs past it, then calls back to a little boy for him to go another way rather than come by it.

OTHER POSSIBILITIES: **3.** Impending health crisis. **4.** Something that has been repressed coming to the surface.

Eye

1. One's outlook or vision.

> Dreamer (male, age 31) is in his father's business office on a Sunday when no one is in the building but the watchman. Dreamer is nervous about being discovered. With a syringe he squirts some liquid into his eyes. The watchman finds him, and punishes him by squirting his eye full of water with a hose.

2. Large eyes: an all-seeing, clairvoyant vision of things.

> Dreamer (male, age 27) is in a graveyard with his brother. The birds there seem to have very large eyes.

OTHER POSSIBILITIES: **3.** Intelligence. **4.** Curiosity. **5.** Personal identity (i.e., "I").

Eyeglasses

1. That which enhances comprehension.

> Dreamer (female, age 45) is back in her childhood home town with her husband, but they are in different houses. She receives two special delivery letters from friends, but cannot find her glasses to be able to read them. The phone rings; it is her husband calling to find out what the letters say.

OTHER POSSIBILITIES: **2.** Clearsightedness. **3.** Mind-set (e.g., "rose-colored glasses").

Falling

1. Conditions (could be physical health, financial, attitudinal/emotional state, etc.) that are falling or may soon go down; can be produced by conscious life fears rather than predictive guidance.

   Dreamer (male, age 30) is at a party. There is a swimming pool in the backyard. Some of his friends play a trick on him and pull him into the pool. He falls to the bottom several times, but each time can rise to the surface again simply by raising his hands.

2. Disappointments in life.

   Dreamer (female, age 46) is falling off the roof of her home. [Note: Cayce interpreted this to mean disappointments soon to come related to individuals in her home life.]

OTHER POSSIBILITIES: 3. Lack of support. 4. Getting caught up in something (e.g., falling in love). 5. Fear of not being in control. 6. Fear of suffering a moral lapse. 7. Fear of falling from or losing a position of prestige.

Feathers

1. Flying feathers: disrupted conditions.

   Dreamer (male, age 48) sees a train with his wife as engineer. It runs into something and he sees feathers flying about from the crash.

2. Plucking feathers: things to be removed so that a new stability can emerge.

   Dreamer (male, age 22) sees people wiring some broken-off branches back onto a tree. Then he sees feathers being plucked. [Note: Cayce interpreted the wired-on branches as new ideas to be grafted on, the feathers as old ones to be removed.]

OTHER POSSIBILITIES: 3. An achievement. 4. A thought or aspiration.

Feet

1. The pathway one is on.

   Dreamer (male, age 55) turns loose an old horse and it climbs a hill. Dreamer walks up behind in the tracks it has made. He's glad it has been shod because its feet now make good tracks for him to use in climbing.

2. Defective feet: flawed pathway one may be following.

> Dreamer (male, age 28) sees a friend whose wife has just given birth to a beautiful child. However, it seems that the baby has defective feet.

OTHER POSSIBILITIES: **3.** Understanding. **4.** Basic assumptions. **5.** Relationship to the ground, to the earth.

Fence

1. Confining oneself by one's own conscious, limited interpretation (or understanding) of things.

> Dreamer (male, age 18) is building a fence with several other people.

2. An enclosure that limits or hedges in.

> Dreamer (male, age 49) has an enclosure (a high wire fence) with all kinds of animals inside: a bear, goat, deer, geese, fox, wolf, and dog. The dog is one he knows in waking life.

OTHER POSSIBILITIES: **3.** Undecided (i.e., "on the fence"). **4.** Barrier. **5.** Difficulty within oneself barring progress or expression. **6.** Protection from outside threat.

Fire

1. Fear that creates a hellish experience.

> Dreamer (male, age 31) sees himself in olden days being burned at a stake by orders of the king. Dreamer is stripped naked and suffers horribly in the flames.

2. A trial that makes things perfect.

> Dreamer (female, age 20) sees a beautiful house on fire. Only the front portion of the house, however, is destroyed. The rear portion is blackened but still standing.

3. Ire (i.e., anger or irritation).

> Same dream as for 2, above. Cayce gave two interpretations for the same symbol in this dream.

4. That which can burn and reduce something (or someone) to nothing.

> Dreamer (female, age 21) sees a dog and a strange fire. [See also DOG, interpretation 2.]

5. Detrimental conditions in the physical body that are consuming.

    Dreamer (male, age 30) sees a lot of oil or gas causing smoke, as if there is a fire and much being destroyed.

6. Temper

    Dreamer (male, age 31) is at a gathering with his mother and other friends. A small fire breaks out. He pays it little attention until it grows to dangerous proportions.

7. Physical conditions that would mar or cause physical distress.

    Dreamer (female, age 48) sees his son standing beside a fire escape window. He tells her bad news about a relative's serious illness.

    OTHER POSSIBILITIES: 8. Passion. 9. Pain.

Fireworks

1. Public acclaim

    Dreamer (male, age 29) is at a party along the oceanfront with family and friends. There is a huge fireworks display.

    OTHER POSSIBILITIES: 2. Achievement and celebration. 3. Dramatic, outer demonstration of one's inner state. 4. Emotional upset.

Fish

1. The Christ.

    Dreamer (male, age 47) is with a friend, near water running over rocks. They are trying to catch fish.

2. A geographic location near water (i.e., where fish can be caught).

    Dreamer (male, age 48) sees a limping old man with a bad foot. He has tied a fish to it, in hopes of getting some relief. Dreamer tries to help him. [Note: This was Edgar Cayce's own dream. The fish symbolized living in Virginia Beach, near the ocean—i.e., a place from which he helped many people through his psychic work.]

3. That achievement to which you may attain.

    Dreamer (male, age 18) is at a pond with his younger brother. There are many fish in the clear-watered pond, despite its muddy bottom. Hornets scare the two away, but finally the dreamer looks for line and hooks in order to go back and catch fish.

4. A lesson that can be drawn out (as a fish is drawn out of water).

Dreamer (male, age 48) is in a boat fishing with friends. There is merriment and an enjoyable time. Some of the people on board are reeling in fish.

OTHER POSSIBILITIES: **5.** Something not quite right (i.e., "fishy"). **6.** Prenatal experience (i.e., life in the waters of the womb). **7.** Ideas and feelings from the inner life. **8.** Dietary recommendation regarding seafood.

Flag

1. National or international affairs/issues (i.e., take note of what kind of flags they are).

Dreamer (male, age 38) is with a business associate at a hospital where they are trying to make sales. Dreamer's father hands him a bag and chickens, with stern instructions to sell them, which he does. There are international flags about. [Note: Cayce's interpretation related the dream to his business sales and international activities.]

2. The standard by which one judges oneself.

Dreamer (male, age 30) sees a flagpole and its flag flying.

OTHER POSSIBILITIES: **3.** Patriotism. **4.** Self-identity. **5.** Call to greater attention toward something.

Flower

1. Hope.

Dreamer (female, age 55) explores the area around a large waterfront home. There is a lake with clear water and swans being fed by happy children, and beautiful flowers all about.

2. Lily: spiritual development, growth, and beauty that grow out of unsightly "muck" (i.e., the lily grows in water and mud).

Dreamer (male, age 27) is looking at a lily when it bursts open and something seems to grow out of it.

OTHER POSSIBILITIES: **3.** Beauty. **4.** Something in oneself about to blossom. **5.** Love. **6.** Growth. **7.** Center of consciousness. **8.** Virginity.

Flying

1. Mastering physical laws and overcoming them; awakening to higher, fourth-dimensional understanding.

Dreamer (male, age 30) is naked and discovers that he can fly. Gracefully, he and others soar about. Then he realizes he has work to do. He flies to a place where a home burglary is happening and tries to talk them out of it.

2. Traveling to be done in the waking state.

   Dreamer (female, age 37) has frequent dreams of flying; no details were given in her reading.

OTHER POSSIBILITIES: **3.** Astral travel or precursor to becoming lucid in a dream. **4.** Desire to avoid something. **5.** Desire to rise above things. **6.** Idealism. **7.** Fantasy or wishful thinking.

Food

1. That which nourishes us spiritually (e.g., truth).

   Dreamer (female, age 58) is handed a cup and a spoon, then goes about feeding people with spiritual food.

2. Anything that sustains us physically.

   Dreamer (female, age 21) refuses to fix lunch for her husband and mother who are both coming home soon.

3. That which sustains and nourishes us mentally (e.g., new ideas or knowledge).

   Dreamer (male, age 31) is at his office and orders from a caterer some rare and unusual food.

4. That with which one feeds the mind.

   Dreamer (male, age 31) sees a baby along a turn in the road. He also sees some food he has prepared for the child.

Foundation (of a building)

1. The physical body of the dreamer (i.e., the "foundation" on which rests the capacity to get anything done).

   Dreamer (male, age 51) goes into a church and sits near the back. He has in hand many papers related to the church service going on. The floor—the foundation of the building—seems to open up and the papers fall through out of his reach.

2. Plans (i.e., on which the possible accomplishments rest).

   Dreamer (male, age 49) is fixing up an old house. He is especially concerned with making a firm foundation. In the rotting parts of the old house he finds dead men's bones.

3. That which is trusted and gives stability to one's life.

> Dreamer (male, age 41) sees an airship with an unusual means of powering itself. Two long bars serve as its foundation and provide a kind of antigravity force.

OTHER POSSIBILITIES: 4. Ideals. 5. Assumptions

Fountain

1. Source from which greater knowledge may be obtained.

> Dreamer (male, age 44) climbs a fence to explore a fountain area and is arrested by military guards. He is taken to a court-martial before a tribunal and he is found guilty.

OTHER POSSIBILITIES: 2. The source of supply. 3. The water of life.

Game

1. Pleasure or enjoyment in a worldly way.

> Dreamer (male, age 30) is on a train with his wife. She is trying to measure something with a croquet mallet, which he thinks cannot be done.

2. Physical efforts or challenges with goals to be made.

> Dreamer (male, age 30) is playing croquet with his father and has only three more wickets in order to win. But he sees that they are three hard ones to make.

OTHER POSSIBILITIES: 3. Childishness. 4. Need for greater exercise or recreation. 5. The "game" of life itself. 6. Competitiveness. [See also GYMNASIUM.]

Giant

1. People or conditions that ridicule or are oppressive to oneself.

> Dreamer (male, age 32) fights with a great giant and things are going badly. Suddenly a small child appears to make a pronouncement and that stops the giant. [Note: Cayce's interpretation was that the giant represented ridicule heaped on the dreamer for having espoused complex spiritual truths—ridicule that makes him feel small. The child shows the solution: present truth in its simplicity.]

2. Conditions that seem to be a hindrance.

> Dreamer (male, age 27) sees a giant leaning over him. It has enormous features, earrings, and a blue towel wrapped around its head.

3. Foreboding of distressing or disagreeable conditions.

   Same dream as for 2, above. Cayce gave a second slant on the meaning of this symbol in this dream.

OTHER POSSIBILITIES: **4.** Strength without wisdom. **5.** Something that has gotten out of proportion.

Glasses (Container for Liquids)

1. That which one holds in mind.

   Dreamer (female, age 21) is at a table, talking with her husband. He criticizes her green water glasses and she tells him to stop it.

OTHER POSSIBILITIES: **2.** Amount of liquid being consumed daily. **3.** Receptivity. **4.** Female sex organs. **5.** All one's inner contents—the soul.

Gloves

1. That which keeps the body warm and healthy (e.g., loss of gloves indicating need to take better care of health).

   Dreamer (male, age 27) is playing in the snow with his brother, as they used to when children. Dreamer slips and falls and drops his gloves. Brother walks away and disappears in a crowd. Dreamer returns home alone and his mother is worried when she sees that his brother isn't with him.

2. Protection.

   Dreamer (male, age 33) is in school with his brother. An ugly, ferocious-looking person appears in the room. The teacher gives dreamer a glove, inside of which is some sort of protection. They all run out into the hall trying to escape.

Golden

1. Truth for the mind.

   Dreamer (female, age 21) sees the backyard of a building and a woman sitting or leaning out of a window. She has wonderful, long golden hair.

OTHER POSSIBILITIES: **2.** Valuable. **3.** Powers of the soul.

Gold Fabric

1. Truths being shown.

   Dreamer (male, age 27) sees the face of a beautiful woman with its expression of love, gaiety, and freedom. She pulls a piece of gold-colored cloth up to her chin.

Golf

1. Exercise for the physical well-being of the body.

    Dreamer (male, age 30) sees himself playing a round of golf.

2. Golf ball: the dreamer or the dream's own life.

    Dreamer (male, age 30) sees a golf ball and golf clubs. Then he recognizes the setting as the 18th hole of a golf course he knows.

3. Golf club: the way one goes about life.

    Same dream as 2, above.

4. Golf course: the world in which we make our way.

    Same dream as 2, above.

Gorge

1. Troublesome conditions along the way.

    Dreamer (male, age 56) is in a car with his wife. He drives through a narrow gorge, over a muddy place where many other cars are stuck, and finally comes to a good road.

OTHER POSSIBILITIES: 2. Obstacles. 3. A situation that has "eroded." 4. Something that calls to the "depths" of oneself.

Grain

1. Knowledge or ideas that can be cast forth for others.

    Dreamer (male, age 49) has many kinds of animals in an enclosure. He is feeding them. He throws grain to them.

OTHER POSSIBILITIES: 2. New ideas that will later bear fruit. 3. Grains in one's own diet. 4. A trifle (e.g., a "grain" of truth). 5. Anything that is physically sustaining.

Green

1. Development; growth.

    Dreamer (female, age 21) is at a table, talking with her husband. He criticizes her green water glasses and she tells him to stop it. [See also GLASSES.]

OTHER POSSIBILITIES: 2. Nature. 3. Receptivity. 4. Envy. 5. Money.

Gun

1. Pistol: aggressiveness, harshness.

> Dreamer (female, age 22) is out walking to school with someone. They find fountain pens scattered along the way, which turn into pistols. Then they must run past some kind of contraption that is about to explode.

2. The source of injury (not necessarily bodily; in this case financial).

> Dreamer (male, age 42) and a companion watch from a mountain cabin porch as one man shoots a rifle at another man. The victim is hit and falls, but gets back up. Time and again he is shot, but he keeps getting up. Finally, one of the bullets hits the dreamer, who is in the line of fire.

3. A way of defending oneself.

> Dreamer (male, age 50) is with a woman who is holding up some men. One of the men grabs her and uses her for protection so no one will shoot him. Dreamer shoots that man in the foot. The bullet travels up his body and out his hand, making him drop his gun.

4. Aiming a gun: keeping properly focused on target or goal.

> Dreamer (male, age 30) is shooting a gun at a target. He's trying hard to improve, and after several shots seems to be getting near the center of the target.

OTHER POSSIBILITIES: 5. Male sex organ. 6. Fear.

Gymnasium

1. School gymnasium: truths being learned in the game of life.

> Dreamer (female, age 21) is back at her college, watching a basketball game in the school gymnasium. She sees that she and all her sorority sisters are dressed alike in uniforms with white dresses and blue ties.

OTHER POSSIBILITIES: 2. Physical exercise. 3. Competitiveness. [See also GAME.]

Hair

1. Reasoning process.

> Dreamer (male, age 27) is combing his hair. He finds that it is knotted and kinked in one place.

2. Thought.

> Dreamer (male, age 30) is sitting on the steps of a university building. An acquaintance comes out and points to his own white hair. His white hair makes him look older, but he is really very much alive and youthful.

3. Knowledge.

> Dreamer (male, age 30) sees an old man with iron gray hair walk by him.

OTHER POSSIBILITIES: **4.** Physical or spiritual strength (e.g., biblical story of Samson).

Hammer

1. The driving force in a situation.

> Dreamer (male, age 48) sees a bull with a funny head, a hammer, and a carpet. [See also BULL.]

OTHER POSSIBILITIES: **2.** Power. **3.** Desire to have an impact. **4.** Building something.

Hat

1. What is currently going on in the life of an individual.

> Dreamer (male, age 30) sees a man with a panama hat on. Dreamer encourages him to wear it turned down all the way around, and he does.

2. The nature of a person's thoughts.

> Dreamer (female, age 21) sees her husband buy two hats. Both look terrible and she tells him so.

OTHER POSSIBILITIES: **3.** Occupation or job undertaken.

Head

1. Functioning of the brain.

> Dreamer (male, age 48) is crazy and looks into his own head. He fixes a wheel in it which had stopped running because of a particle of dirt or trash that had gotten in.

2. An attitude, orientation, or way of approach (e.g., dream character with head on backward means approaching things in backward fashion).

> Dreamer (male, age 54) sees a Chinese girl with her head on backward.

3. Headless: inability to reach that person through normal, physical, conscious means; can only be contacted through spiritual means.

Dreamer (male, age 32) sees his father's and uncle's bodies dug up out of the grave. But the heads are missing. Despite the hideous sight and smell, the dreamer begins to preach to them, and they seem to listen to him in spirit.

4. Headless: warning not to lose your head in daily duties.

Dreamer (male, age 27) sees a headless man in the uniform of a sailor, walking in an erect manner with either a gun or cane in his hand. [See also UNIFORM.]

OTHER POSSIBILITIES: 5. Conscious intentions. 6. Intelligence. 7. Directive force.

Hole

1. A faulty condition in oneself.

Dreamer (female, age 48) has shoes that hurt her feet terribly. She takes them to a shoemaker who fixes them. But she sees that she has holes in her stockings. [See also SHOES.]

OTHER POSSIBILITIES: 2. Something missing. 3. An opening to something new. 4. Entrance to the unconscious. 5. Female sex organ. 6. The whole (i.e., a pun).

Home/House

1. Condition and effects created by one's current work in life.

Dreamer (male, age 48) is in a beautiful, large home—and yet it has a dismal, dark entrance. A friend comes to the door to announce that his son has died at college and asks if the coffin could temporarily be placed here in the dreamer's home. Soon the body arrives in its casket.

2. The "place" in which one dwells in consciousness (i.e., one's state of consciousness).

Dreamer (male, age 29) is in a large house in a southern resort area with his family members. A party is going on in a nearby room and the dreamer wonders about being a part of it.

3. The mental state of an individual.

Dreamer (male, age 30) sees an oceanfront house being built by one man alone. He hears the words, "Let your wife attend to that." [Note:

Cayce's interpretation was that the dreamer's mental orientation toward doing things independently should be tempered by letting others be of assistance.]

4. Back of house—hidden portion of one's mental state.

Dreamer (female, age 20) sees a beautiful house on fire. Only the front portion of the house, however, is destroyed. The rear portion is blackened but still standing.

OTHER POSSIBILITIES: 5. Spiritual home. 6. Domestic life. 7. The body. 8. The personality. 9. Front of house: the facade shown to the world. 10. Basement—unconscious or instincts.

Hornet, Wasps

1. Troublesome obstacles to be overcome.

Dreamer (male, age 18) is at a pond with his younger brother. There are many fish in the clear-watered pond, despite its muddy bottom. Hornets scare the two away, but finally the dreamer looks for line and hooks in order to go back and catch fish.

2. Warning about dangerous condition (i.e., may be painful).

Dreamer (male, age 49) sees a woman who has changed herself into a pig in order to keep others from seeing her. She and dreamer feel a sexual attraction and they go into a house to be alone. But they are discovered in their naked condition as they go in, and in defense turn themselves into a horsefly (dreamer) and a wasp (woman).

Horse

1. The messenger.

Dreamer (male, age 55) turns loose an old horse and it climbs a hill. Dreamer walks up behind in the tracks it has made. He's glad it has been shod because its feet now make good tracks for him to use in climbing. [Note: Cayce's interpretation sees the horse here as the Messenger or the Christ, in whose steps we are to follow.]

2. The message and the messenger.

Dreamer (male, age 30) watches a horse race in which especially strong, spirited horses outclass the rest of the field. They run so swiftly and powerfully that they throw from their backs the black jockeys riding them. A huge crowd looks on at this wild race which, at the end, is in a storm and rain.

3. The nature of the message may be represented in the kind of horse (e.g., a charger, a slow workhorse, a racehorse, etc.).

Dreamer (male, age 49) sees a number of different horses and their riders.

OTHER POSSIBILITIES: **4.** Making progress. **5.** Unbridled emotions. **6.** Instincts.

Intruder

1. Breaks into home: the breaking of a law; the breaking of a spiritual law (because the home represents the spiritual home).

Dreamer (female, age 22) is in her childhood home with her mother. They hear intruders and go upstairs to investigate. Three men have broken in—not to steal, but to enquire about leaving liquor at their house.

2. Self-indulgent attitudes or behaviors.

Dreamer (female, age 21) is on a streetcar going to college. She gets off with two other women and a man, who stalks her. She stays near the other two—safety in numbers. Eventually the man changes into someone who helps her with her school problems.

OTHER POSSIBILITIES: **3.** A threatening and avoided side of oneself. **4.** The "shadow" or ignored side of oneself.

Key

1. The conscious knowledge necessary to understand more of the Universal Laws (i.e., the "lock" represents the mysteries of living in a material world).

Dreamer (male, age 30) is trying out several keys to open a lock. Finally he finds the right key and works the lock open.

2. Safety or that which provides safety.

Dreamer (male, age 29) takes some keys off his dresser at home and puts them in his pocket. Then he takes some money off his dresser and also puts it in his pocket.

3. The solution or answer to a situation.

> Dreamer (male, age 31) has a new business partner who is evaluating his recent transactions in the stock market. Two lines are strung across the room from which two keys hang. Dreamer knows they were given as a token for each 100 shares of a certain stock purchased.

King

1. The attainment of a high goal.

> Dreamer (male, age 31) has been given a mathematical problem to solve, but the method to use escapes him. Then he is shown the same problem in a practical application—the example of a king on his throne, carved out of wood.

OTHER POSSIBILITIES: 2. Help, assistance, and aid that can come from beyond oneself. 3. What you are ruled by. 4. God. 5. The dominant idea in your mind. 6. The side of yourself you consider most majestic. 7. Earthly power. 8. Your own father or his influence on you.

Knife

1. A "two-edged" tool that can be used either for defense, or to force one's own way upon another.

> Dreamer (male, age 31) is at school and gets into a fight with someone. Dreamer stabs his antagonist with a small knife and then is stabbed in return. Even though he overcomes his opponent, the sight of all that blood distracts him and drives him insane.

2. Forces exerted in the material world for destruction.

> Dreamer (male, age 29) had dream interpreted by Cayce without the actual dream being read to him or recorded.

OTHER POSSIBILITIES: 3. Male sex organ. 4. Aggressiveness; hostility. 5. Piercing mind.

Ladder

1. The Way (i.e., the ladder to heaven).

> Dreamer (female, age 44) is climbing a ladder and near the top notices that a rung is missing. Only with great difficulty is she able to overcome this problem and reach the top. Others, coming up the ladder, don't seem to be so impeded by this.

2. Missing rung of ladder: a hardship along the way of life.

Same dream as immediately above; the Cayce reading offered two aspects of an interpretation for the same symbol in this dream.

3. Any kind of ascent.

Dreamer (male, age 30) sees a girl he thinks he remembers from college days. To his surprise and pleasure she remembers him, too. He asks if she knows how to climb a certain nearby ladder, and she proceeds to lead the way by climbing it with him.

4. Descending a ladder: doing something in life that is a "step down" from what was previously done.

Dreamer (male, age 32) sees a friend on a rooftop who comes down a stepladder in a hurry.

OTHER POSSIBILITIES: **5.** Success. **6.** Improvement that comes through a series of separate events or efforts. **7.** Elevated social prestige.

Lake

1. Peace and tranquility.

Dreamer (female, age 55) explores the area around a large waterfront home. There is a lake with clear water and swans being fed by happy children. There are beautiful flowers all about.

OTHER POSSIBILITIES: **2.** A haven. **3.** Pool: that which reflects or mirrors. **4.** The unconscious mind. [See also WATER.]

Leaves

1. Dead leaves on ground—that which is sloughed off or ejected (like dross from the physical body).

Dreamer (male, age 55) sees a little mound of dead leaves that seems to move. He assumes there is a snake under it and approaches with a stick in hand. The snake pokes its head out and says: "Don't hit me. I won't bother you anymore."

OTHER POSSIBILITIES: **2.** Life; growth. **3.** Easily blown about or separated from one's origins. **4.** That which provides shade or relief from intensity.

Letter

1. Information that comes.

   Dreamer (male, age 31) sees a postman enter his office with a special delivery letter. He hopes it is from Edgar Cayce for him, but is disappointed to see it is addressed to someone else.

2. Messages of truth.

   Dreamer (female, age 45) is back in her childhood hometown with her husband, but they are in different houses. She receives two special delivery letters from friends, but cannot find her glasses to be able to read them. The phone rings. It is her husband calling to find out what the letters say.

OTHER POSSIBILITIES: 3. A realization. 4. Telepathic contact.

Light

1. Great lessons and great truths.

   Dreamer (female, age 48) sees the heavens open up and a great, powerful light envelops her.

2. Knowledge and its application that brings understanding.

   Dreamer (male, age 19) sees a light with four beams shooting out of it: one gray, one dark, one black, and one very light. [Note: Cayce's interpretation suggested that different phases or degrees of knowledge and application are depicted by the four different beams.]

3. The throne of God's presence.

   Dreamer (female, age 21) sees an old man with a gray beard dressed in pure white like a sheep. She is greatly impressed. The man pulls the dreamer's mother by the arm, out into the light.

4. The rays of God's love, peace, and happiness.

   Dreamer (male, age 30) is in a darkened room where he sees a box with a light inside it. The light is revolving on a tripod, throwing its beams all about.

5. A higher force and power.

   Dreamer (male, age 32) sees a round sort of light of darkened hue, set rather high up. He knows it to be another consciousness, and it speaks to him. It is the Christ.

6. That directing force as would show the way to gain more perfect knowledge.

   Dreamer (male, age 30) sees many shining lights, each of which he knows is a discarnate spirit-being. He senses that one is his deceased father. The dreamer's wife suggests that he turn out the electric light in the room; and upon doing so, his father appears in bed with him. The dreamer cries from the intense emotion of this reunion, and they exchange affirmations of love for each other.

7. Hope.

   Dreamer (male, age 27) sees the mother of his sister-in-law in her hospital room [in waking life she was actually ill]. It is night and she has a new night nurse. A ray of light comes in from the corner of the room; it pulsates stronger, then weaker.

OTHER POSSIBILITIES: **8.** One's conscious awareness of individuality. **9.** Conscious intellect. **10.** Conscious attention.

Light Bulb

1. That which brings the light of understanding.

   Dreamer (male, age 32) is on board an ocean liner with family and friends. One person tells him a dream about being chased by lighted lamps all around the house. The dreamer interprets this symbol for the woman: the lighted lamps mean truth and understanding that she was trying to get.

2. One's own intuition.

   Dreamer (male, age 31, who is a stockbroker in waking life) goes into a darkened bathroom. On the floor he finds the light bulb, which has fallen out of the socket. As he looks at it, he hears his brother's voice tell him he shouldn't have sold a particular stock.

Lightning

1. The higher forces, which may be destructive to many people, but can be a life-giving flow.

   Dreamer (male, age 30) is struck by lightning under a tree.

2. Fear.

   Dreamer (female, age 22) is struck by lightning.

OTHER POSSIBILITIES: **3.** Sudden realization. **4.** Revenge. **5.** Sudden discharge of tension. **6.** Instant karma.

Liquor

1. Laying aside physical consciousness (i.e., liquor being a way of altering consciousness).

    Dreamer (female, age 22) is in her childhood home with her mother. They hear intruders and go upstairs to investigate. Three men have broken in—not to steal, but to enquire about leaving liquor at their house.

2. Literally, about drinking habits.

    Dreamer (male, age 28) sees a leak of liquor out of a bottle or keg onto the foyer rug of his home. [Note: Cayce's interpretation was a warning about greater discretion in drinking habits.]

OTHER POSSIBILITIES: **3.** Dissolved inhibitions. **4.** Intoxication; ecstasy. **5.** The spirit (pun). **6.** Temporary relaxation. **7.** Desire to escape reality.

Luggage

1. That which you "have in hand" in your life.

    Dreamer (male, age 50) is at a train station about to leave on a trip. He puts his luggage down outside, along with that of other passengers. When he looks back later, his luggage is gone. In his concern he looks for it, only to then miss the train.

2. That which is at hand and is "tried and true."

    Dreamer (male, age 48) is on a train trip. He then comes to a hotel where he is given the opportunity to exchange his old, well-worn luggage for luggage that is shining and new.

OTHER POSSIBILITIES: **3.** Burdens, psychological or physical.

Marriage

1. An inner union with the higher forces that opens creativity.

    Dreamer (male, age 32) sees his grandmother, who leads him away by the hand. She says, "Here comes the bride. The bride cometh to the groom."

2. Commitments to be honored in regard to another person (not necessarily just the spouse).

    Dreamer (female, age 22) is about to marry her cousin, but she is hesitant. She hems and haws, undecided about what to do.

3. Duty to be kept.

Dreamer (male, age 30) finds himself married to an acquaintance, but it is not wholly acceptable or pleasing to him. [Note: Cayce's interpretation was to do his best and fulfill his duties in many areas of life, even when conditions aren't exactly as he might like.]

4. Close relations with another person that bring goodness and happiness (but not necessarily a literal marriage).

Dreamer (male, age 30) gets a reading from Cayce that instructs him to get a cottage for himself and his wife in a certain neighborhood. It also instructs his mother to get married and take the house next door.

5. The inner marriage with the Christ.

Dreamer (female, age 44) sees a marriage ceremony with a big red apple on the altar. [Note: Cayce's interpretation was that the apple represented a sacrifice to be made—her judgmental attitude toward others—so that her inner marriage with the Christ could happen.]

6. A business deal, a joining of commercial interests.

Dreamer (female, age 45) and a close personal friend are in a train station, waiting to catch their train and go on a trip. This friend is soon to be married and they are also here awaiting the arrival of the groom. But their train arrives before his comes in, and they decide to get on theirs, hoping he will follow soon.

OTHER POSSIBILITIES: **7.** A unifying of two aspects of one's own personality. **8.** Initiation.

Maze

1. Confusion in the face of many turning points or options.

Dreamer (male, age 32) is in a theater, which becomes a room with many doors and a maze of different turning points.

OTHER POSSIBILITIES: **2.** Emotionally disorganized.

Mirror

1. How one is seen by others.

Dreamer (male, age 32) sees a mirror set at such an angle that only by getting into a certain position could he see himself reflected.

OTHER POSSIBILITIES: **2.** Self-examination. **3.** Self-reflectiveness, self-consciousness of one's own individuality. 4. Narcissism. 5. Maya; illusion; that which isn't real but only a reflection.

Money

1. Benefits or returns from efforts.

> Dreamer (male, age 49) is in a dilemma. The ruler of some oriental country (in a warm climate) has died, and the only way the dreamer can help his people is to marry the former ruler's daughter. This country is prepared to pay considerable money to the dreamer's wife and children to compensate them so that this marriage can happen. [Note: Cayce's interpretation pointed to the dreamer's plan to take a trip to Florida and the considerable financial benefit that might come from the trip.]

2. The vehicle (or channel) for making exchange.

> Dreamer (male, age 29) takes some keys off his dresser at home and puts them in his pocket. Then he takes some money off his dresser and also puts it in his pocket.

3. Borrowed money: favorable conditions that have strings attached (i.e., obligations).

> Dreamer (male, age 30) is lifting himself up on a horizontal bar to peer over a wall. He pulls himself up, saying to himself: I'm going into this using borrowed money, but I'll soon be able to pay it back. [Note: Cayce's interpretation was that getting an advantaged position—i.e., lifting oneself up—with borrowed resources also has obligations.]

4. That which is of value and truth.

> Dreamer (male, age 30) is giving out dollar bills to people as they come past him one by one.

5. A criterion or a way of indicating success.

> Same dream as 4, above.

6. Sign of appreciation for services rendered.

> Dreamer (female, age 21) is at the movies with her husband. They both receive a huge amount of money for the services they have given.

7. An opportunity to make money (literally).

> Dreamer (male, age 43) is approached by his business partner, who wants to use an empty bottle. When the dreamer goes to his basement

to get one, he surprisingly finds a pile of money. [Note: Cayce's interpretation concerned money to be made in business from a bottled product.]

8. Necessity to raise considerable money: warning about becoming extravagant.

Dreamer (male, age 18) has a business partner and they need to raise some money. They know just the man to go to, but they also know that he is difficult to get to see.

9. Worthless paper money: warning about gambling.

Dreamer (male, age 42) is on a crowded streetcar going to a prizefight. At the arena there is a mob rush to get tickets, but the dreamer arrives at the ticket window first. To pay for his ticket he pulls out worthless foreign paper money.

10. The material world and its values.

Dreamer (male, age 31) is on a boat talking with his deceased father, who now is back in the flesh. The dreamer asks him about the nature of life in the spiritual world. He is told it has no money or thermometers (to measure weather).

11. Million dollars: promise that whatever resources (not just money) are required will be supplied as the need arises.

Dreamer (male, age 30) is suddenly very wealthy. He has a million dollars and buys a large house for Edgar Cayce and his psychic work.

OTHER POSSIBILITIES: 12. Power, authority, strength. 13. Time and/or energy. 14. Love. 15. Counterfeit money: phoniness; cheating; insincerity.

Moon

1. Carnal romance, the impulse to earthly passion.

Dreamer (male, age 31) is sexually attracted to a woman. He deserts his wife and marries this other woman. But his father denies that his actions can be justified. Dreamer sees the moon shining down through broken clouds, and then a voice criticizes his actions.

OTHER POSSIBILITIES: 2. Sentimentality. 3. The irrational realm of feelings. 4. Feminine. 5. Intuition. 6. The unconscious soul. 7. Madness (i.e., "lunacy"). 8. Menstrual cycle. 9. Desire, yearning.

Mountain

1. Reaching higher and higher in mental development.

    Dreamer (female, age 53) and a companion are climbing a mountain. They get separated and dreamer cannot find her.

2. A place from which there is a more perfect understanding of the physical world.

    Dreamer (male, age 18) is riding with someone to the top of a high mountain. At the top he is shown a beautiful view.

3. A place where an understanding of truth is gained.

    Dreamer (male, age 29) leaves a crowd of people and climbs a mountain. On the way up he encounters difficulties and is fearful of robbers.

4. Gaining the full height or the full concept of a matter.

    Dreamer (male, age 31) is on a mountaintop with his father. They discuss the options that the dreamer has in his business life, and his father gives him some advice.

5. The rise to the spiritual forces.

    Dreamer (male, 43) tries to escape the rising waters of a tidal wave with his family. They go up to a mountain summit and find a church. With the water at their heels they start to scale the walls of the church.

OTHER POSSIBILITIES: **6.** Highly idealistic, but still with one's feet on the ground. **7.** Obstacles and difficulties (if one is atop the mountain, then these are overcome). **8.** Exaggerations (e.g., making a mountain out of a mole-hill). **9.** Ambitions. **10.** Climbing mountain: first half of life; descending mountain: second half of life.

Movies

1. Mass consciousness; the attitudes of the populace at large.

    Dreamer (female, age 21) is at the movies with her husband. They both receive a huge amount of money for the services they have given.

OTHER POSSIBILITIES: **2.** The story of one's own life.

Mud

1. That which makes for a hindrance.

    Dreamer (male, age 56) is driving a car with his wife as a passenger. They drive through a narrow passage, around obstructing rocks, over a muddy place where many other cars have gotten stuck, and finally come to a good road and nearby clear water.

OTHER POSSIBILITIES: 2. The retarding aspect of one's own hesitations and fears. 3. That which, despite appearances, can contain a treasure or can aid healing (e.g., Jesus sometimes used it). 4. Stuck or caught up in something. 5. Excrement. 6. The womb; one's own origins. 7. Neglect. 8. Abuse of the body.

Newspaper

1. Comics: encouragement to use one's sense of humor and laugh more often.

> Dreamer (male, age 30) is reading the comics section of the Sunday paper while Edgar Cayce lies nearby in a trance state for a reading. Dreamer laughs and thinks that there is humor in psychic work, too.

OTHER POSSIBILITIES: 2. Public attention. 3. Common knowledge. 4. New realization, new information. 5. Prophecy.

Nudity

1. Fleshly desires.

> Dreamer (male, age 49) sees a woman who has changed herself into a pig in order to keep others from seeing her. She and dreamer feel a sexual attraction and they go into a house to be alone. But they are discovered in their naked condition as they go in, and in defense turn themselves into a horsefly (dreamer) and a wasp (woman).

2. The uncovering or exposure of something intended to be kept hidden.

> Same dream as for 1, above. Cayce gave two interpretations for the same symbol in this dream.

3. Ignorance or not understanding (i.e., "that bareness . . . to which [one] is reduced, by not opening self to an understanding . . .").

> Dreamer (male, age 18) is building a fence with others. But then he loses his trousers and other clothing, and he must ask others to help him with this predicament.

4. Feeling one is laid bare to criticism; vulnerable in this fashion.

> Dreamer (female, age 21) goes to a store to purchase a dress. She changes clothes in a dressing room, but notices that all the people could see her with her clothes off.

OTHER POSSIBILITIES: **5.** Stripped of the "masks" one wears in relating to the world. **6.** A desire for others to know one's real feelings. **7.** Humility. **8.** The refusal to keep playing a role in life.

Old Man/Old Woman

1. Wisdom through many experiences, the seer or sage.

> Dreamer (male, age 30) sees an old man with iron-gray hair walk by him.

2. Christ symbol.

> Dreamer (female, age 21) sees an old man with a gray beard dressed in pure white, like a sheep. She is greatly impressed. The man pulls the dreamer's mother by the arm, out into the light.

OTHER POSSIBILITIES: **3.** Old lesson learned that now needs new application in a new way. **4.** One's past. **5.** Karma. **6.** Worries about growing old.

Orchestra

1. Harmony among the forces of one's life.

> Dreamer (male, age 30) sees an orchestra, all playing different instruments and dressed in white. They are playing in perfect harmony.

OTHER POSSIBILITIES: **2.** The importance of music in one's life. **3.** One's emotional nature.

Pants

1. Changing: changing one's personal philosophy of life.

> Dreamer (male, age 30) is at his temple listening to a sermon. He takes off his pants to change into some different ones, but this is noticed by others and creates an embarrassing disturbance.

OTHER POSSIBILITIES: **2.** Sexual feelings and desires (i.e., to cover the lower part of the body). **3.** Authority, leadership (e.g., who wears the pants in the family?).

Parents

1. Those who are available to give aid and assistance.

> Dreamer (male, age 30) is riding on top of a moving car, but he begins to slip and his position is precarious. His parents are inside the car as passengers.

OTHER POSSIBILITIES: **2.** Father: one's own father or feelings toward him. **3.** Father: the energetic, protective side of God. **4.** Mother: one's own mother or feelings toward her. **5.** Mother: the receptive, nurturant side of God.

Party

1. One's social life.

Dreamer (male, age 30) leaves a party attended by friends and family members. He goes looking for the Spirit-Light of his deceased father, but along the way he finishes drinking a bottle of whiskey from the party. A voice warns that he won't find his father in this environment.

2. A special development in one's education or mental growth.

Dreamer (female, age 21) is at a house party with many other college friends. She decides she wants to leave and catches a bus.

3. The physical diet when too many sweets are being consumed.

Dreamer (male, age 31) is at a party eating refreshments. Two other party-goers start a fistfight and the dreamer separates them.

OTHER POSSIBILITIES: **4.** Gaiety. **5.** Lack of depth or meaning.

Pawnshop

1. Trading off in a way that wastes valuable resources.

Dreamer (male, age 30) goes to a pawnshop and sells his precious Sunday school medal for what seems to be an amazing amount— $800. He tries to give a false name to the pawnbroker.

Pen/Pencil

1. A way of thinking.

Dreamer (male, age 27) is wearing his brown suit coat and it gets dirty from a big ink stain on the lapel when his fountain pen leaks. He feels the suit is ruined.

OTHER POSSIBILITIES: **2.** What one has been writing or encouragement to write. **3.** Male sex organ.

Perfume

1. A person's particular, unique attitudes and ways of expression in the world.

Dreamer (female, age 21) sees bottles of different perfumes in front of her.

OTHER POSSIBILITIES: **2.** Emotional reactions. **3.** Attempts to cover up or present in a better light. **4.** Psychic influence.

Pig

1. Sexual desires.

> Dreamer (male, age 49) sees a woman who has changed herself into a pig in order to keep others from seeing her. She and dreamer feel a sexual attraction and they go into a house to be alone. But they are discovered in their naked condition as they go in, and in defense turn themselves into a horsefly (dreamer) and a wasp (woman).

2. "Hogs" the whole show.

> Dreamer (male, age 48) tries to drive a pig back through a gate into its proper place, from which it has escaped.

OTHER POSSIBILITIES: **3.** Greedy. **4.** Stubborn (i.e., pig-headed). **5.** Gluttony.

Platform

1. Shaky and unstable: the condition of one's physical body is weakened or imbalanced.

> Dreamer (female, age 21) is going swimming from a rickety platform—very unsubstantial in its structure. She dives in and makes a belly-whopper and it hurts.

OTHER POSSIBILITIES: **2.** One's appearance before others (e.g., "on stage" or "on your soapbox").

Pocket

1. Something kept for oneself rather than distributed.

> Dreamer (male, age 29) takes some keys off his dresser at home and puts them in his pocket. Then he takes some money off his dresser and also puts it in his pocket.

OTHER POSSIBILITIES: **2.** Memory. **3.** Inner reserves (e.g., of vitality, abilities, money, etc.). **4.** Possession. **5.** Receptivity. **6.** The female sex organs.

Poison

1. Danger, detrimental conditions warned of.

> Dreamer (male, age 27) is approached by a man selling a radio. Then someone puts poison on the doorknob of the dreamer's door and tries

to force him to touch it. [Note: Cayce's interpretation warned about a business deal involving radio stocks.]

OTHER POSSIBILITIES: **2.** Improper diet that is toxic to the body. **3.** Problems with one's own physical eliminations creating toxicity. **4.** Attitudes or emotions that are harming oneself and/or another.

Police

1. The law, especially universal or spiritual laws.

Dreamer (female, age 21) is at gambling tables with her husband and friends. A policeman comes in and breaks up the games. But then a plainclothes policeman enters and says it is all right to continue. Finally, the uniformed policeman returns and breaks up the games once and for all, arresting people. [Note: Cayce's interpretation included the suggestion that the plainclothes policeman symbolizes the law interpreted from merely a human, fleshly level.]

2. That which tries to bring disorder under control.

Dreamer (female, age 21) is in a house with her mother. It begins to storm outside, and a wild man is running through the streets shooting his gun. They rush to close and lock their windows. Policemen are chasing and trying to catch the wild man.

OTHER POSSIBILITIES: **3.** Inhibitions. **4.** Conscience. **5.** Higher, protective forces. **6.** Karmic law. **7.** Guilt.

Priest

1. Safety, security, and strength in the spiritual forces.

Dreamer (male, age 43) is with other family members and they are trying to escape the rising waters of a tidal wave. They climb a hill, finding some religious buildings. A priest waves them toward the best place to climb to escape the water.

OTHER POSSIBILITIES: **2.** Minister or rabbi—personal feelings toward such spiritual leaders, including associations from childhood. **3.** One's own inner spiritual authority. **4.** Conscience. **5.** The desire to be virtuous.

Prisoner

1. Being controlled by outside conditions.

Dreamer (male, age 18) is a prisoner of a very strong man who wrestles with him and hurts him. The man and his servant lie across a bed, their heads hanging over the edge, and feed a pet turtle. Dreamer sneaks up and chops off their heads with an ax.

2. Trapped in efforts to justify oneself (misusing the mind in this way).

Dreamer (male, age 30) is at a gathering where someone identifies himself as a Ku Klux Klan member. He and the other Klansmen take dreamer and others as prisoners. They march them away, but dreamer escapes and is chased by one Klansman.

3. Prison: trapped by lazily letting one's life be too centered in one direction (i.e., imbalanced).

Dreamer (male, age 20) and his family are helping someone escape from a prison. Dreamer's role includes the task of leaving the escape car and going into the prison camp.

OTHER POSSIBILITIES: 4. A side of oneself trapped by a sense of inadequacy, fear, or guilt. 5. Someone else in the dreamer's life who is trapped by conditions.

Pulling

1. Pulling oneself up: raising one's own position to a more advantageous one.

Dreamer (male, age 30) is lifting himself up on a horizontal bar to peer over a wall. He pulls himself up, saying to himself: "I'm going into this using borrowed money, but I'll soon be able to pay it back." [Note: Cayce's interpretation was that getting an advantaged position—i.e., lifting self up—with borrowed resources also has obligations.]

OTHER POSSIBILITIES: 2. Strong emotional attraction. 3. Strong influence (i.e., a pun on having "pull").

Pulpit

1. Leadership; teaching aptitude.

Dreamer (male, age 31) sees himself in a pulpit where he is making predictions for the people of Israel.

OTHER POSSIBILITIES: 2. Spiritual healing. 3. Spiritual teachings. 4. Religious life.

Radio

1. One's own capacity to attune or tune in to better understandings (even to higher forces or psychic forces).

Dreamer (male, age 31) is in his childhood home with his mother and brother. They are listening to radio programs, but can only get local stations. Dreamer fails in his efforts to make adjustments to bring in more distant stations.

2. The way in which the Father can "hear at a distance" our needs.

Dreamer (male, age 31) is visited at home by God, in the form of an honest, intelligent businessman. Dreamer welcomes God into his home and talks with him; however, his brother and mother are listening to the radio and don't pay much attention.

3. Our capacity to attune to the Infinite and receive a power that manifests in physical life.

Same dream as for 2, above. Cayce gave two interpretations for the same symbol in this dream.

4. Force and power that can radiate a far distance.

Dreamer (male, age 31) sees a younger brother who is building an elaborate radio system, with many parallel aerials and elaborate decoration.

OTHER POSSIBILITIES: 5. Entertainment. 6. The body's own sense of hearing. 7. Communication with others. 8. Public knowledge. 9. Telepathy.

Rain

1. Blessings, benefits.

Dreamer (male, age 30) watches a horse race in which especially strong, spirited horses outclass the rest of the field. They run so swiftly and powerfully that they throw from their backs the black jockeys riding them. A huge crowd looks on at this wild race which, at the end, is in a storm and rain.

2. Conditions that are coming down.

Dreamer (male, age 31, who is a stockbroker in waking life) is at his office and notices out the window that it is raining. He wonders about the up or down movement of the market that day.

OTHER POSSIBILITIES: 3. Emotions and the release of feelings. 4. Sadness or grief. 5. Obstacles. 6. Cleansing process. 7. Deliverance from a dry spell. 8. Need to drink more water.

Red

1. Desires of the heart.

> Dreamer (male, age 30) tells his brother that he would like to transfer from Columbia to Yale, but then he realizes that he cannot fulfill this desire because of business commitments that keep him in New York. They watch a football game. One player stands out because he has on a red jersey, whereas everyone else on his team wears blue.

2. Meaningful; important to be understood or grasped.

> Dreamer (male, age 30) receives a typewritten copy of a reading from Cayce. Certain portions of it are underlined in red ink.

3. Blood.

> Dreamer (male, age 30) sees a red-and-white striped pencil. [See also BLOOD; PEN/PENCIL.]

4. Trouble or misunderstanding.

> Dreamer (male, age 8) sees three little wagons, one of which is red.

5. Red hat: higher attributes of mind development.

> Dreamer (male, age 30) is on a tennis court. A man tells him that he cannot talk while playing. A woman with a large, red hat tells him the same thing. Dreamer responds, "I'll bet you one dollar I can play, talk, and beat you."

OTHER POSSIBILITIES: 6. Passion. 7. Anger. 8. Sexual desire. 9. Energy. 10. Stop.

Restaurant

1. Food for the body's physical needs.

> Dreamer (male, age 30) is in a restaurant and sees a woman eating a big cherry pie. He orders one too but is told they are all gone. Instead he orders cake, which the waitress throws at him in anger.

2. A place of seeking the higher foods of spiritual growth (i.e., "feed at the table of the Giver of all good and perfect gifts").

> Dreamer (male, age 31) is seated in a big, high chair at a restaurant table. His companions are seated at a lower level and they are all eating and happy.

OTHER POSSIBILITIES: 3. Sociability.

River

1. The way of life.

> Dreamer (male, age 30) sees two ways to cross a river: an upper bridge and a lower bridge. He takes the lower one, which goes right along the edge of the water and seems a bit dangerous.

2. Stream: a dividing line.

> Dreamer (male, age 48) is walking through a beautifully kept garden area with a veiled woman. They cross a stream of water and are met by the messenger Mercury. He unites them in a ceremony and then they start up a steep hill that they must climb.

OTHER POSSIBILITIES: **3.** The source of fertility. **4.** The current of one's energies. **5.** The passage of time.

Road/Path/Street

1. The journey of life one is on.

> Dreamer (male, age 44) is walking to a meeting at night. It is through hilly country and he takes a high road, but notices another traveler taking a low road.

2. Rough, poor roadbed: troublesome conditions to be encountered.

> Dreamer (male, age 30) is with a business associate on a trolley car. He notices the roadbed for the trolley. It is good for a way, but becomes very poor.

3. Junction, crossroad: choices in life about how to use resources.

> Dreamer (male, age 31) is walking down a road and picks up a gilded sword. Ahead he sees a commotion of many people at a crossroads. Firemen turn hoses on the crowd to disperse them. The owner of the sword—a lieutenant—comes up and demands it back. Dreamer feels rebuked and hurt but obediently gives it back with a joking manner.

4. Junction, crossroad: a time in life when one especially needs guidance.

> Dreamer (male, age 31) is at a crossroads and he sees his wife. He recognizes some trouble in relationships with her and/or with his own mother. He gives his wife a Bible to carry.

OTHER POSSIBILITIES: **5.** The direction one is pursuing. **6.** One's destiny.

Rocks

1. Large ones in a road: troublesome conditions along the way.

> Dreamer (male, age 56) is driving a car with his wife as passenger. They drive through a narrow passage, around obstructing rocks, over a muddy place where many other cars have gotten stuck, and finally come to a good road and nearby clear water.

2. Difficulties to overcome.

> Dreamer (female, age 47) is in a large, beautiful field near a cemetery with her husband. He is shoveling a large pile of rocks into a small cart.

OTHER POSSIBILITIES: 3. Boulders: sturdiness and stability. 4. Latent strength. 5. Emotional sterility (e.g., "heart of stone" or "stony silence"). 6. Earthiness.

Roof

1. The top or pinnacle of thought and understanding.

> Dreamer (male, age 30) is on the rooftop of a house, looking up to the sky and questioning the nature of reality.

2. Hanging from edge of roof: getting oneself into precarious situations or circumstances.

> Dreamer (male, age 33) is hanging onto a roof. At first it seems that he will have a lot of trouble getting down, but he doesn't.

OTHER POSSIBILITIES: 3. Protection; security; shelter; nurturance.

Rubbish/Trash

1. Disorder and laxness in life.

> Dreamer (female, age 53) and a friend walk by a house near the beach that is owned by Edgar Cayce. Dreamer remarks that the tenants don't pay their rent. There is much old and new rubbish all around.

OTHER POSSIBILITIES: 2. Ideas of little value or meaning. 3. Toxins or waste products of the physical body that need to be eliminated.

Runner

1. That force through which the individual may gain strength to go alone.

> Dreamer (female, age 45) is running up a road with a man and woman. All three are in bathing suits. Anytime dreamer tires in running she

can hold onto the man, rest momentarily, and then keep running on her own. They arrive at a large pool of water in which there are many shells and people swimming.

OTHER POSSIBILITIES: 2. A need for more exercise. 3. A part of oneself trying to avoid something. 4. Feeling hurried. 5. Strong commitment and desire to get to a goal.

Scar

1. A deficiency resulting from a past condition.

> Dreamer (male, age 30) is in an argument over finances with his mother, father, and grandmother. His father takes charge of leading the discussion and dreamer notices a scar on the side of his forehead.

2. From operation: reminder of how it is sometimes necessary to have something removed (i.e., particularly from the mind).

> Dreamer (male, age 31) watches his father take a bath after an appendectomy operation. As he gets out of the tub, dreamer sees the scar.

OTHER POSSIBILITIES: 3. Memory of a painful experience. 4. Lasting impact on the mind.

School

1. The issues of daily life.

> Dreamer (female, age 21) sees herself back at her college just after graduation. She is put off and is critical of the insincerity of the girl who was class president.

2. The lessons or training to which the mind may attain.

> Dreamer (male, age 31) is in an advanced school, yet not in one of the upper grades. He has difficult classes and burdensome amounts of homework, but the teacher decides to lighten the reading load.

3. One's own teaching of others.

> Dreamer (male, age 30) is in a Sunday school building that has been set afire purposely by one teacher. Many students are trapped and killed because teachers, rabbis, and preachers have locked all exits. Dreamer barely escapes, then angrily confronts the teacher who started the fire and learns his reason: he was upset because of student insults. [Note: Cayce interpreted the dream as related to dreamer's

own overreactions to criticism when he is communicating or teaching his ideas.]

4. Higher learning; learning about universal laws.

Dreamer (male, age 49) sees a school building where classes have been recessed for recreation.

OTHER POSSIBILITIES: **5.** Unresolved issues from one's own school years. **6.** The desire to learn.

Scissors

1. Seeming opposites that, when applied for truth, can accomplish much.

Dreamer (male, age 30) is cutting his fingernails with scissors as he talks to his brother and a friend. They are discussing the relative worth of science and religion.

OTHER POSSIBILITIES: **2.** The desire to cut loose from something. **3.** Cutting remarks; cynicism. **4.** Feeling cut off from someone else or a part of oneself. **5.** Hostility.

Scorpion

1. That which is dangerous or poisonous.

Dreamer (male, age 32) and his brother are with two uncles who are skeptical about psychic work. They receive a package that contains a scorpion. Dreamer carefully attaches a piping arrangement to it and draws out fluids, which are to be used to cure the disease of one uncle.

OTHER POSSIBILITIES: **2.** Bitterness. **3.** Stinging, hurtful attitudes or remarks.

Seed

1. That which is able to bring forth into manifestation something of its own kind (e.g., like begets like). [Note: No dream; Cayce offered this as a universal interpretation.]

2. The word of truth.

Dreamer (male, age 31) is following a narrow path that leads into a room with many doors. He purposefully sticks to a course that leads through a certain door—the one that leads on the other side to a seed.

OTHER POSSIBILITIES: **3.** The stored experience of the past that leads to new possibilities. **4.** An ideal. **5.** Offspring (physical or nonphysical). **6.** New beginnings.

Servant

1. The reminder to be of service (i.e., as in "He who would be greatest or master must be servant to all").

> Dreamer (male, age 31) hears the announcement of the maid servant that God Himself is at the front door of his house. Sure enough, God comes in, looking not like a clergyman but like a robust, intelligent businessman.

OTHER POSSIBILITIES: **2.** Those qualities in oneself that are fully under control and able to be purposefully directed. **3.** Obedience.

Shanty/Shack

1. Humility, lowly estate.

> Dreamer (male, age 30) is out in the country in a little shanty house with his brother and sister-in-law. Dreamer agrees that he will never be as wealthy as his brother, but his thoughts turn to how nonmaterial things make him most happy.

OTHER POSSIBILITIES: **2.** Physical body out of balance. **3.** Impoverished state of mind.

Shells

1. The many different forms or physical manifestations that come from the original oneness (i.e., the sea).

> Dreamer (female, age 45) is walking along the ocean. She sees various kinds of fish and many people, in and out of the water. She gathers many different kinds of seashells.

2. Individuals who may be helped or missed in the passage of daily life (i.e., just as one may notice or miss a seashell on the beach).

> Dreamer (female, age 45) is in a large department store with a friend, where they see a large pool of water. It has many seashells in it, but she doesn't gather any because of a railing around the pool.

3. Great truths that have been gathered.

> Dreamer (female, age 45) is running up a road with a man and woman. All three are in bathing suits. Anytime dreamer tires in running she

can hold onto the man, rest momentarily, and then keep running on her own. They arrive at a large pool of water, in which there are many shells and people swimming.

OTHER POSSIBILITIES: **4.** One's tendency to crawl inward for self-protection. **5.** Hardness. **6.** Beauty.

Shepherd

1. The leader. [Note: no dream; Cayce volunteered an interpretation of this symbol in one reading.]

OTHER POSSIBILITIES: **2.** Nurturance. **3.** The Christ.

Shirt

1. The thought or intent taken toward others.

> Dreamer (male, age 45) is working on a special motor he is creating. His shirt gets dirty, so he changes it. While he does, the motor disappears, seemingly taken right in front of his face. [Note: Cayce warned that this invention might be stolen from him if his attitudes toward others weren't proper.]

2. The attitudes and understandings of life that one "wears."

> Dreamer (male, age 30) is wearing a new blue-striped shirt. He thinks it looks pretty, but a voice tells him to look at it more closely.

OTHER POSSIBILITIES: **3.** Feeling, emotions, passions. **4.** Financial resources (e.g., "losing your shirt").

Shoemaker

1. The source of *assistance* in formulating a foundation (shoes) for one's life.

> Dreamer (female, age 48) has shoes that hurt her feet terribly. She takes them to a shoemaker, who fixes them. But she sees that she has holes in her stockings.

Shoes

1. An individual's foundation.

> Dreamer (female, age 48) has shoes that hurt her feet terribly. She takes them to a shoemaker, who fixes them. But she sees that she has holes in her stockings.

OTHER POSSIBILITIES: **2.** Basic principles. **3.** Protection from physical life. **4.** Sole of shoes—pun on the word "soul." **5.** A person's role in life or identity (e.g., "to be in his shoes").

Silhouette

1. Looking at things with a one-sided, limited view.

> Dreamer (male, age 27) sees a cut-out silhouette of a human face in profile.

OTHER POSSIBILITIES: **2.** Something only dimly understood. **3.** The shadow or unconscious side of oneself.

Snake

1. The wisdom of all things.

> Dreamer (male, age 55) sees a little mound of dead leaves that seems to move. He assumes there is a snake under it and approaches with a stick in hand. The snake pokes its head out and says: "Don't hit me. I won't bother you anymore."

2. Temptations.

> Same dream as 1, above. Cayce gave two interpretations for the same symbol in this dream.

3. That which threatens harm.

> Dreamer (male, age 56) sees a big snake curled up in his wife's lap.

4. Those who would harm in an underhanded manner.

> Dreamer (male, age 30) is in the woods with his mother and wife. They see a mean-looking snake and run in panic. By following his mother's example of running a zigzag course, they all escape successfully.

5. Monstrous and hissing: self's own condemnation of self.

> Dreamer (male, age 30) is in a college bookstore where he sees a hissing snake. He tries to get away from it, but it keeps confronting him. Dreamer feels hedged in and wants to get free.

OTHER POSSIBILITIES: **6.** Kundalini; pure creative energy. **7.** Self-transcendence (i.e., sheds its own skin). **8.** Paradox (e.g., good/evil; wisdom/temptation). **9.** Sexuality.

Spider

1. A menace; a warning about a threat, about getting caught in a web.

   Dreamer (male, age 55) is troubled by a large spider that makes huge webs inside the dreamer's home. He thinks he's killed it, but it reappears and makes another large web outside the house. He knocks it to the ground and hacks it to pieces with his knife.

   OTHER POSSIBILITIES: 2. Entrapping, smothering behavior (often, but not always, associated with a mother or other feminine figure).

Spoon

1. Do things in small doses.

   Dreamer (female, age 59) is handed a cup and a spoon, and then feeds people with spiritual food.

   OTHER POSSIBILITIES: 2. One's station in life (e.g., "born with a silver spoon in her mouth"). 3. Calling attention to diet.

Stage

1. To make something public, to allow the outside world to see.

   Dreamer (male, age 30) sees a chorus of girls dancing on a stage.

   OTHER POSSIBILITIES: 2. The desire to be in the limelight. 3. A point of development (i.e., a pun on "stage of development"). 4. The center of one's present attention or interest.

Statue

1. A part of oneself that is lifeless, but which may awaken and come to life.

   Dreamer (female, age 41) sees a miniature statue of an adult. It seems to be alive. She feels joyful holding it in her arms.

2. The physical product of that which is created first as a mental image.

   Dreamer (male, age 31) is frightened to see a marble statue standing right next to his bed where he is resting. He tries to reassure himself by saying that the statue is only a reflected image of lights on the ceiling.

3. An image to show the "formulative spirit" or spirit that emanates (e.g., the Statue of Liberty represents the spirit of a nation).

   Dreamer (female, age 26) travels on a ship to New York, where she sees the Statue of Liberty.

OTHER POSSIBILITIES: 4. How one aspect of self has been molded by someone else. 5. Unfeeling; unresponsive. 6. Someone who has been "put on a pedestal." 7. A wish to keep alive the memory of a deceased person.

Step/Stairs

1. An ascent in knowledge or a better understanding gained little by little. Dreamer (male, age 32) sees a woman with two children, one dead and the other dying. He tries, using mind power, to bring the soul of the dead child back. Then he and the dreamer climb steps.

OTHER POSSIBILITIES: 2. Changes in consciousness. 3. After-death state; heaven. 4. Stages of work ahead.

Stick

1. Represents the rod or staff of life.

> Dreamer (male, age 55) sees a little mound of dead leaves that seems to move. He assumes there is a snake under it and approaches with a stick in hand. The snake pokes its head out and says: "Don't hit me. I won't bother you anymore."

2. Sign of authority of the leader.

> Same dream as 1, above. Cayce gave two interpretations for the same symbol in the dream.

OTHER POSSIBILITIES: 3. Discipline. 4. Male sex organ.

Stripes

1. Something subject to change (i.e., as opposed to solid color that shows a consistency).

> Dreamer (male, age 27) is in a conversation in which he compares white silk pajamas to blue-striped pajamas of another material.

OTHER POSSIBILITIES: 2. Level of achievement (e.g., stripes on a military uniform). 3. Feeling trapped (e.g., prisoners traditionally wear striped clothing). 4. Variety.

Sun

1. The spiritual force which presents lessons or knowledge (i.e., the sunshine).

> Dreamer (male, age 30) is in an apartment with others, in a room into

which sunlight streams through the window. That seems nice, but the room starts getting warmed too much that way. He'd rather go to another room, seemingly inaccessible to him, where he knows his father to be.

2. The Father's love to all.

Dreamer (male, age 30) sees a beautiful landscape of mountains and a river. The sun shines down brightly on it. He feels a closeness to God.

OTHER POSSIBILITIES: **3.** Life and energy. **4.** Happiness and success. **5.** Need to get outside in the sun more often. **6.** The source. **7.** Intellect; rationality. **8.** The masculine. **9.** The Christ.

Swan

1. Peace and serenity.

Dreamer (female, age 55) explores the area around a large waterfront house. There is a lake with clear water and swans being fed by happy children. Beautiful flowers are all about.

OTHER POSSIBILITIES: **2.** The soul.

Swim

1. Submerged in or attuned to universal forces.

Dreamer (female, age 22, pregnant) is in India, where she sees many streams flow together into a pool of water. She jumps in and swims, saying to her husband, "You see, it does not hurt my pregnant condition to do this."

2. Making headway in some endeavor.

Dreamer (male, age 30) is in New York's Central Park where he sees some teachers in a rowboat on a lake. They are laughing at him and it reminds him of his childhood, when he was a bit slow academically. Then he goes into the lake and swims very fast, to the admiration of those same people in the boat.

OTHER POSSIBILITIES: **3.** Coping with one's feeling nature. **4.** Feeling buoyed up, confident. **5.** Sexuality.

Sword

1. The Spirit (like a two-edged sword that can cut either way).

Dreamer (male, age 31) is walking down a road and picks up a gilded sword. Ahead he sees a commotion of many people at a crossroads.

Firemen turn hoses on the crowd to disperse them. The owner of the sword—a lieutenant—comes up and demands it back. Dreamer feels rebuked and hurt but obediently gives it back with a joking manner.

2. Power and authority.

Same dream as 1, above. Cayce gave two interpretations for the same symbol in the dream.

OTHER POSSIBILITIES: **3.** War; antagonism. **4.** Discrimination; discernment. **5.** Strength of character. **6.** Protection. **7.** Masculine sexuality.

Teacher

1. Anything that aids the development of the mind.

Dreamer (male, age 31) is in an advanced school, yet not in one of the upper grades. He has difficult classes and burdensome amounts of homework, but the teacher decides to lighten the reading load.

OTHER POSSIBILITIES: **2.** Authority figure. **3.** One's own talent to teach. **4.** The conscience within. **5.** Someone who is critical, demanding, or testing.

Teeth

1. Spoken words.

Dreamer (female, age 22) faints on a busy city street. She falls and knocks out several teeth.

2. False teeth: sharp words recently spoken.

Dreamer (female, age 20) is with her sister-in-law, who says that she will have to get all false teeth.

3. False teeth that shone like pearls and gold: these unreasonable-appearing teeth represent speech that is only "show" and takes the place of real application.

Dreamer (female, age 21) sees an acquaintance whose false teeth look remarkable: they shine like pearls, some are gold and are of different shapes with pretty edges.

OTHER POSSIBILITIES: **4.** The maturing process (e.g., one's teeth fall out and are replaced at certain stages of childhood). **5.** Eating; diet. **6.** Getting involved with something or someone (e.g., "getting your teeth into it"). **7.** Effectiveness; potency (e.g., "toothless" means ineffective, impotent).

Telephone

1. A way of gaining information.

Dreamer (male, age 30) is at his business office where a new telephone has been installed. To call other cities requires careful use of a complicated dialing mechanism. He goes upstairs to tell a business associate about this new telephone, and this man shows him something else—a telescope.

2. A coming message.

Dreamer (female, age 21) hears the telephone ring in her home. She goes to answer it, saying loudly so her husband will hear it: "Don't you hear the telephone ringing?"

OTHER POSSIBILITIES: **3.** Communicating with others. **4.** Telepathy. **5.** One's own intuition.

Telescope

1. The capacity to perceive things far off (i.e., the future).

Dreamer (male, age 30) is at his business office where a new telephone has been installed. To call other cities requires careful use of a complicated dialing mechanism. He goes upstairs to tell a business associate about this new telephone, and the associate shows him something else—a telescope.

OTHER POSSIBILITIES: **2.** Clearer insight. **3.** Sensitivity to the nature of seemingly small things (i.e., small incidents). **4.** Making something big out of something small.

Temple

1. Assistance in understanding one's own spiritual welfare.

Dreamer (male, age 30, Jewish) is with his wife and a crowd of wealthy, influential people, most of whom are boisterous and drunk. First the dreamer, then the whole crowd, decides to go visit the temple. They go in the back door and sit in a pew. Peaceful organ music is playing.

2. Past-life memory of an incarnation working in a temple.

Dreamer (female, age 38) is wandering through a temple, seeking the counsel of the person in charge. She gets lost in a crowd; a fire interferes with her passage. Finally, she finds a seat among those in power there.

3. The spiritual forces that come into play with the conscious mind in studying any subject.

> Dreamer (female, age 20, Jewish) sees her mother-in-law in a temple.

OTHER POSSIBILITIES: 4. The physical body. 5. One's feelings and attitudes toward religion.

Tent

1. An insecure dwelling (i.e., a place in consciousness that is not fixed, secure, stable).

> Dreamer (male, age 27) is in a tent. Looking up toward one corner, he gives some orders to God.

OTHER POSSIBILITIES: 2. Attitude of changeability. 3. Temporary protection.

Thermometer

1. Measurements or judgments made using a physical-world standard.

> Dreamer (male, age 31) is on a boat talking with his deceased father, who now is back in the flesh. Dreamer asks him about the nature of life in the spiritual world. He is told there is no money nor thermometers (to measure weather).

OTHER POSSIBILITIES: 2. Measurement of one's emotional state. 3. Warning about possibility of future ill health.

Train

1. Train ride: the journey of life.

> Dreamer (male, age 31) is on a train ride to a major city. As they draw near their destination the train starts making many local stops in the suburbs to pick up more passengers.

2. Taking a trip (literally).

> Dreamer (male, age 50) is at a train station about to leave on a trip. He puts his luggage down outside, along with that of the other passengers. When he looks back later, his luggage is gone. In his concern he looks for it, only to then miss the train.

3. Engineer of train: the directing, controlling force in some life situation.

Dreamer (male, age 43) sees his wife as the engineer of a train. It runs into another car and feathers fly all about.

4. Stock exchange trading of train stocks.

Dreamer (male, age 48, stockbroker) is on a train trip. He then comes to a hotel where he is given the opportunity to exchange his old, well-worn luggage for luggage that is shining and new.

5. The necessity to get moving, to grow and change.

Dreamer (male, age 30) sees a train on which he is going to make a journey. There is some talk of needing to be vaccinated.

OTHER POSSIBILITIES: 6. Train tracks: orthodoxy, the accepted way of doing things. 7. An opportunity (e.g., "missing the train"). 8. A series of thoughts. 9. Vitality. 10. Following the proper course (i.e., "on track"). 11. Victimized; punished unfairly (i.e., "railroaded").

Trip

1. Changes that will come.

Dreamer (female, age 21) is on a boat trip with her husband. There is considerable shouting and fighting on board. Finally, the boat is struck by lightning and the whole boat explodes. It sinks and they are killed.

2. Actual trip to be taken soon.

Dreamer (male, age 18) stays at home while his mother and father go off on a trip. Visitors come to the house and dreamer has a good time with them.

3. Mental changes happening (i.e., in attitudes).

Dreamer (male, age 20) is on a car trip with his family. Just after leaving he stops to help a man in a fight. Later he stops again to buy fireworks.

OTHER POSSIBILITIES: 4. The journey through life. 5. One's destiny.

Turban

1. That which is mysterious to the mind.

Dreamer (female, age 21) is shopping for a new dress with her mother. Dreamer has her hair arranged like a turban. She tries on a dress, which the saleswoman says is pretty; but her mother and another saleswoman disagree.

OTHER POSSIBILITIES: **2.** Psychic powers or fortune-telling.

Turtle

1. The strength of new life; longevity.

Dreamer (male, age 18) is a prisoner of a very strong man who wrestles with him and hurts him. The man and his servant lie across a bed, their heads hanging over the edge, and feed a pet turtle. Dreamer sneaks up and chops off their heads with an ax.

2. Slow.

Dreamer (male, age 31) is treated in a drugstore by a doctor for his sore toe. She rubs on a salve made of turtle shell. Other people in the store are all eating ice cream and sodas. [Note: Cayce's interpretation was that eating too many sweets was slowing down proper activity of digestion and blood supply.]

OTHER POSSIBILITIES: **3.** Methodical. **4.** Introverted; tending to withdraw into a "shell." **5.** Encouragement to move slowly.

Uniform

1. Dressed in a uniform: one's duty.

Dreamer (male, age 27) sees a headless man in the uniform of a sailor who is walking in an erect manner with a gun or cane in hand. [Note: Cayce's interpretation was to see a pun in the symbology: don't lose your head in the service and duties you perform.]

2. A shared or common trend of thought (i.e., among all who wear the same uniform).

Dreamer (female, age 21) is back at her college, watching a basketball game in the school gymnasium. She sees that she and all her sorority sisters are dressed alike in uniforms, with white dresses and blue ties. [See also GYMNASIUM.]

OTHER POSSIBILITIES: **3.** Vocation or profession. **4.** Conformity; orthodoxy. **5.** Authority and power (e.g., a policeman in uniform has authority). **6.** Subservience (e.g., when one wears a military uniform he must serve his superiors).

Wading

1. Taking on a new experience slowly and prudently.

Dreamer (male, age 27) is at the oceanfront beach. He goes out into the waves. But instead of wading out, he immediately dives into a breaker. His head goes right into the sand. He's stuck and almost suffocates as friends try to pull him out.

OTHER POSSIBILITIES: **2.** Childhood; childishness. **3.** Timidness.

Wagon

1. Intents, purposes, and desires in life.

Dreamer (male, age 8) sees three little wagons, one of which is red.

OTHER POSSIBILITIES: **2.** The means by which one moves through the journey of life. **3.** The physical body. **4.** Sobriety (e.g., "on the wagon").

Wall

1. An obstacle to be overcome (climbed) before the goal/ideal can be attained.

Dreamer (male, age 48) and a female companion must together climb over a wall on their way up a mountain hillside.

2. The challenge to apply a truth; the moment of truth (e.g., "up against a wall," where one must do something that makes or breaks a situation).

Dreamer (female, age 48) watches as a condemned man escapes just before he is to be hanged. He flees into the crowd that gathered to see his execution. He crawls very rapidly to avoid detection and to get away, but finally bumps his head and is stopped by a brick wall.

OTHER POSSIBILITIES: **3.** Confinement. **4.** Protection and shelter.

Water

1. The mother of all living organisms.

Dreamer (female, age 45) is running up a road with a man and woman. All three are in bathing suits. Any time dreamer tires in running she can hold onto the man, rest momentarily, and then keep running on her own. They arrive at a large pool of water, in which there are many shells and people swimming.

2. The source of physical creation: Mother Sea.

> Dreamer (female, age 45) is walking along the ocean. She sees various kinds of fish and many people, in and out of the water. She gathers many different kinds of seashells.

3. The cleansing force as one moves from one experience to another.

> No dream; Cayce offered this interpretation as one universal meaning.

4. The mother of life.

> No dream; Cayce offered this interpretation as one universal meaning.

5. The source of life and understanding.

> Dreamer (male, age 55) is wading into water with two close friends. Dreamer steps into a place where the water goes over his head. He yells for help and they try to assist him.

6. The beginning or source of all forces.

> Dreamer (female, age 22, pregnant) is in India, where she sees many streams flow together into a pool of water. She jumps in and swims, saying to her husband, "You see, it does not hurt my pregnant condition to do this."

7. Life or the living way.

> Dreamer (male, age 29) is at a party along the oceanfront with family and friends. There is a huge fireworks display.

8. Clear water: clearness of understanding, purity of purpose.

> Dreamer (male, age 56) is driving a car with his wife as passenger. They drive through a narrow passage, around obstructing rocks, over a muddy place where many other cars have gotten stuck, and finally come to a good road and nearby clear water.

9. Dirty water: imperfect understanding and knowledge.

> Dreamer (male, age 27) is bathing. The water runs off him in dirty streams.

10. The water of Life as found in Christ.

> Dreamer (male, age 48) takes a dead child from a casket. Holding her close to his body for warmth, she seems to be resuscitated. She asks for a drink of water and he finds a cedar bucket of water for her. The girl doesn't want to go back to her former home and dreamer says she can stay with him.

11. The first element of life.

> Dreamer (male, age 30) sees his wife swimming across a large body of water. It is dangerous, but her goal is to reach a man standing on the cliff at the opposite shore. She makes it across and hands a silver cup (like a trophy cup) to the man, who has now become the dreamer himself.

OTHER POSSIBILITIES: **12.** Feelings, moods, and desires. **13.** Need for more water to be drunk. **14.** The soul. **15.** The unconscious. **16.** The realm of the feminine. **17.** Birth and/or death.

Wave (Sea)

1. Conditions that are wavering.

> Dreamer (male, age 30) and others are on a boat coming into a harbor. They see another boat struck by a huge wave that knocks sailors overboard. Then the waters grow calmer and those sailors climb back aboard.

OTHER POSSIBILITIES: **2.** Waves of emotion.

Weeds

1. Neglect.

> Dreamer (male, age 49) sees two acquaintances who are cleaning grass and weeds from a plot of land that has become overgrown while they were away. They say they are to open a bookstore on that place.

OTHER POSSIBILITIES: **2.** That which chokes out desired growth.

White.

1. Purity.

> Dreamer (female, age 21) sees herself in a blue-and-white dress, kneeling in prayer before a doctor who has helped treat her sick mother. She says a prayer of thanks to him and God.

OTHER POSSIBILITIES: **2.** Innocence. **3.** The ideal of completeness. **4.** Weakened.

Wild Man

1. Emotional upset (e.g., uncontrolled anger).

> Dreamer (female, age 21) is in a house with her mother. It begins to storm outside, plus a wild man is running through the streets shooting

his gun. They rush to close and lock their windows. Policemen are chasing and trying to catch the wild man.

OTHER POSSIBILITIES: **2.** Fears. **3.** An ignored and repressed side of oneself.

Woods/Forest

1. A mental place where one can easily get lost or confused, such as in the maze (of trees).

Dreamer (female, age 21) walks through a woods with her husband and other family members. They are to prepare dinner when they arrive at their destination. One person in the group finds a long cabinet and opens it. There is a skeleton inside and most of them run in fear. Looking back, however, they see that it's really a loaf of bread.

OTHER POSSIBILITIES: **2.** The unconscious mind. **3.** Nature, or the encouragement to get out in nature.

SELECTED
BIBLIOGRAPHY

Harmon H. Bro. *Edgar Cayce on Dreams*. New York: Warner Books, 1968.

Edgar Cayce. *The Edgar Cayce Readings: Dreams and Dreaming Parts I and II*. Virginia Beach, VA: A.R.E. Press, 1976.

Gayle Delaney. *Living Your Dreams*. San Francisco: Harper & Row, 1980.

Sigmund Freud. *The Interpretation of Dreams*. New York: Avon Books, 1965.

Celia Green. *Lucid Dreaming*. London: Hamish Hamilton, 1968.

C. G. Jung. *Memories, Dreams and Reflections*, edited by Aniela Jaffe. New York: Random House, 1961.

C. G. Jung. *Modern Man in Search of a Soul*. New York: Harcourt, Brace and World, 1933.

Frederick Perls. *Gestalt Therapy Verbatim*, edited by John O. Stevens. Lafayette, CA: Real People Press, 1969.

Henry Reed. "Dream Incubation: A Reconstruction of a Ritual in Contemporary Form," *Journal of Humanistic Psychology*. Fall 1976.

Henry Reed. *Getting Help from Your Dreams*. Virginia Beach, VA: Inner Vision Publishing, 1986.

G. Scott Sparrow. *Awakening the Dreamer*. Virginia Beach, VA: A.R.E. Press, 1978.

G. Scott Sparrow. *Lucid Dreaming: Dawning of the Clear Light*. Virginia Beach, VA: A.R.E. Press, 1976.

Montague Ullman and Stanley Krippner, with Alan Vaughn. *Dream Telepathy*. New York: Macmillan, 1973.

Montague Ullman and Nan Zimmerman. *Working with Dreams*. Los Angeles: Tarcher, 1979.

INDEX

This index does not include entries from part four.

Aesculapius, 134
Altered states of consciousness, 31
Archetypal symbols. *See* Types of dream
  symbology, universal or archetypal
Astral body, 108; leaving dream body,
  116; shells, 115
Astral plane, 114; aging on, 115; within
  self, 116
Astral projection, 107–14; highest form
  of, 116; warnings concerning, 113–
  15
Aura, 108
Awakening the Dreamer (Sparrow), 87

Borderland, 100–102

California, 110
Causes of dreams, 8, 41, 45, 70, 73;
  desire, 72–73; fear, 72, 74–75;
  indigestion, 3
Cayce, Edgar (the man), xiii, 43–44,
  75–76, 97; as a dream symbol, 100,
  123; his dreams, 98, 107; his
  perception of auras, 108; past life
  dream, 131
Cayce, Gertrude, 44, 75, 107, 123
Chicago, 106

Christ, 11–12, 98–99, 113
Conscious mind, 30, 38, 61, 68, 75, 78,
  123
Creativity, 13

Death, 100–102; after-death
  experience, 9; astral plane, 114
Definitions of dreams, 8, 23; a contact
  with God, 11; instructions, 12; a
  look into the future, 13–14;
  problem solving, 12, 13; real
  experiences, 9; symbolic picture, 10
Delaney, Gayle, 87–88, 134
Dream dictionaries, xv, 84, 96, 141;
  creating your own, 85–86, 142;
  how to use, 85, 90, 141;
  limitations, 78, 83, 86, 141–142
Dream interpretation defined, 37
Dream journal, 27, 32–34, 49, 125;
  preparation for guidance, 134
Dream recall, 23–25
Dream recall techniques, 25; bedtime
  reading, 26; discussion groups, 31;
  dream recording materials, 27; go
  to bed early, 26; life inventory, 29;
  lounge in bed, 28–29; prayer and
  meditation, 30–31; presleep

suggestion, 27; recording feelings
when no dreams, 30; relive in
reverse, 29–30; review your
purposes, 26; wake up at night, 28
Dream reverie, 16–18
Dreams: business advice, 79, 83;
compensatory, 68–69, 110; lucid,
5, 103, 106, 114, 116; past-life,
127–32; physical health, xiii, 5–6,
13, 70–72, 74, 133; recurrent, 43–
44, 101; retrocognition, 127–32;
terrifying, 3; wish fulfillment, 73,
124
Dream symbology (other than
alphabetized entries in part four),
9–10, 37–38, 47–48, 50, 105;
airplane, 45; arsonist, 81;
automobile, 6; baby, 53; backyard,
20; ball, 48; blood, 45, 85; bottle,
79; brother, 82; cave, 20; cliff, 44–
45; crash, 45; dog, 107; drugstore,
72; elephant, 84; flagpole, 45;
food, 21; giant, 86–88; head, 76;
light, 98; liquid, 57; liquor, 79;
messenger, 44; money, 79;
mountain, 20, 45; play on words,
75–77; prizefight, 43; railroad
train, 42; shirt, 127; sister, 81;
starch, 76; water, 21, 84; wild man,
83
Dream theme, 48. *See also* Simple story
line

Ego, 38
Egypt, 131
ESP in dreams, xiii, xiv, 21, 81, 118;
precognition, 4, 9, 13–14, 53, 74,
123–127; telepathy, 4, 5, 119–23
Etheric body, 108

Fables, 55–56
Fairy tales, 55–56
Fear, explained by a dream, 130. *See
also* Causes of dreams, fear
Feelings changed by a dream, 10
Flying in dreams, 103–5
Freud, Sigmund, 37–38, 73
Future, 123–24, 132; dream symbols
indicative of, 125

Galileo, 128
Gestalt therapy, 89
God, 11, 30, 73, 95, 98, 117
Great Pyramid, 117
Greece, ancient, 133–34
Group work on dreams, 31
Guidance in dreams 13–14, 53, 63, 65–
68, 70, 72–73, 75, 129, 132;
decision-making, 133; evaluation,
114, 123, 136–37; incubation,
133–37; need for evaluation, 102

Heading Toward Omega (Ring), 109
Heaven, 114
Howe, Elias, 13
Hypnogogic state, 27

Ideals and purposes, 12, 26, 44–45,
100, 112–14, 127
Individuation, 38
Ingredients of a dream, 18; dream title,
18; literal references, 21; opening
scene, 19–20; personal symbology,
21; simple story line, 22; universal
symbology, 20
Inventories, life, 13, 24, 40–41

Jesus, 98, 116
Jones, Sam, 98
Jung, Carl, 37–38, 68, 78, 86, 88

Kansas City, 106
Kirlian photography, 108

Life After Life (Moody), 109
Living Your Dreams (Delaney), 87
Love, 101–2, 106, 112, 116; continuity
after death, 115
Lucid dreaming. *See* Dreams, lucid

Mary, the mother of Jesus, 99, 133
Meditation, 31, 112
Moody, Dwight, 98
Moody, Raymond, 109
Multiple levels of meaning, 42–43

Near-death experience, 109
New York City, 94

Nightmares, 3, 70
Norfolk, Virginia, 123
North Carolina, 109, 111

Out-of-body experience, 107–15

Parables, 55–56, 59–60
Perls, Fritz, 89
Prayer, 5, 31
Presleep suggestion, 26
Puns, 75–77; as a past-life indicator, 132

Rapid eye movement (REM), 23
Reed, Henry, 24, 134
Reincarnation and the purpose of past-life dreams, 128
Relationships, 11, 21, 29, 31, 40, 66; continuity after death, 101, 115; family, 9–10, 12, 39, 71, 130–31; romantic, 58, 73, 121–22, 129; warning about, 127
Ring, Kenneth, 109

Simple story line: definition of, 47–48; examples of, 22, 65–76, 82, 85–86, 94; format, 54–57, 60–61; guidelines for writing, 49–54
Sleep, 26–27, 108
Sleep laboratories, 23
Soul, xiii, 9, 38, 100–102; after death experience, 115; communication, 114; its psychic nature, 118; memory, 129, 131

Sparrow, G. Scott, 87
Spiritual world, 9
Stevenson, Robert Louis, 13
Subconscious mind. *See* Unconscious mind
Suicide, 119–20
Symbols, definition of, 78. *See also* Dream symbology

Tibet, 117
Time, 29, 132
Titling a dream, 32
Types of dream symbology: emblem, 80–83, 89; signs, 79; universal or archetypal, 20, 83–84, 89. *See also* Dream symbology

Unconscious mind, 27, 38–39, 41, 68, 73, 78, 80, 90; all subconscious minds are in contact, 120, 122; nature of time, 132; subconscious, 124; suggestions to the subconscious, 134–35
Universal symbols. *See* Types of dream symbology, universal or archetypal

Van de Castle, Robert, 134
Virginia Beach, Virginia, 123
Visions, 97

Warnings in dreams, 124, 126–27
Will, 13, 73, 105

ABOUT THE
AUTHOR

Mark Thurston, Ph.D., is an educator, author, and administrator for the Association for Research and Enlightenment, founded in Virginia Beach, Virginia, by Edgar Cayce in 1931. Thurston's ten publications include *Edgar Cayce Predicts, Understand and Develop Your ESP, The Inner Power of Silence, Experiments in Practical Spirituality,* and *The Paradox of Power.* His academic training in psychology provides skills for translating concepts from the Cayce readings into modern daily life.

Thurston's personal and professional study of dreams spans twenty years. In addition to one previous book about dreams, he has also led dream interpretation workshops in virtually every major city in America and Canada.

EDGAR CAYCE'S
WISDOM FOR THE NEW AGE

More information from the Edgar Cayce readings is available to you on hundreds of topics from astrology and arthritis to universal laws and world affairs because Cayce established an organization, the Association for Research and Enlightenment (A.R.E.), to preserve his readings and make the information available to everyone.

Today over sixty thousand members of the A.R.E. receive a bimonthly magazine, *Venture Inward*, containing articles on dream interpretation, past lives, health and diet tips, psychic archaeology, psi research, book reviews, and interviews with leaders and authors in the metaphysical field. Members also receive extracts of medical and nonmedical readings and may do their own research in all of the over fourteen thousand readings that Edgar Cayce gave during his lifetime.

To receive more information about the association that continues to research and make available information on subjects in the Edgar Cayce readings, please write A.R.E., Dept. M13, P.O. Box 595, Virginia Beach, VA 23451, or call (804) 428-3588. The A.R.E. will be happy to send you a packet of materials describing its current activities.